letters to a young actor

Also by Robert Brustein

The Theatre of Revolt

Seasons of Discontent

The Play and Prose of Strindberg (editor)

The Third Theatre

Revolution as Theatre

The Culture Watch

Critical Moments

Making Scenes: A Personal History of the Turbulent Years at Yale

Who Needs Theatre

Reimagining American Theatre

Dumbocracy in America

Cultural Calisthenics

The Siege of the Arts: Collected Writings 1994–2001

Adaptations of Drama

The Father, by August Strindberg

The Sea Gull, by Anton Chekhov

The Cherry Orchard, by Anton Chekhov

The Master Builder, by Henrik Ibsen

When We Dead Awaken, by Henrik Ibsen

Six Characters in Search of an Author, by Luigi Pirandello

Robert Brustein

letters to a young actor

a universal guide to performance

A Member of the Perseus Books Group
New York

Dedicated to the Company of Actors

Hardcover published in 2005 by Basic Books
A Member of the Perseus Books Group
Paperback published in 2007 by Basic Books

Books published by Basic Books are available at special discounts for bulk purchases in the United States by corporations, institutions, and other organizations. For more information, please contact the Special Markets Department at the Perseus Books Group, 11 Cambridge Center, Cambridge MA 02142, or call (617) 252-5298 or (800) 255-1514, or e-mail special.markets@perseusbooks.com.

Library of Congress Cataloging-in-Publication Data
Brustein, Robert Sanford, 1927–
Letters to a young actor : a universal guide to performance / Robert Brustein.
p. cm.
Includes index.
ISBN-13: 978-0-465-00806-3; ISBN-10: 0-465-00806-2 (alk. paper)
1. Acting—Vocational guidance. I. Title
PN2055.B78 2005
792.02'8'023—dc22

2004023438

Paperback ISBN-13: 978-0-465-00814-8
Paperback ISBN-10: 0-465-00814-3

10 9 8 7 6 5 4 3 2 1

Contents

1 Prologue

Dear Young . . .

But what shall I call you? If we are going to spend time together as writer and reader, you must have a name. Are you male or female, gay or straight? What generic title can appropriately identify the variety of genders and types you represent? Faced with a similar dilemma, Shakespeare made Rosalind take the name of Zeus's cup bearer, Ganymede, after she had put on tights and traveled to the Forest of Arden in *As You Like It.* And Viola, in Shakespeare's other major pants role, decided to call herself Caesario after a similar metamorphosis from feminine to masculine in *Twelfth Night.* Shakespeare's plays are full of sexual ambiguity (so is his poetry—in the Sonnets, he calls his patron the "master-mistress of my passion"). Perhaps it will be simplest just to call you by the name Chekhov used in his letters to Olga Knipper, the woman who later became his wife: "Dear Actor."

Well, then, dear young Actor, permit me to play a part, too—your guide in this book—and walk you through your career on the stage; we'll begin at the very beginning, when you first thought about becoming an actor, move through college and advanced training to your first steps as a performer, then, finally, arrive at your evolution as a fully fledged member of the acting profession.

I have made this trip with hundreds of young people since I first started training actors at the Yale School of Drama in 1966. I look forward to renewing that journey with you.

I.

Starting Out

2

Inching into the Profession

Where shall we start, dear Actor? Perhaps with the question everybody asks at one time or another: Why act? Why, indeed. Those who achieve wealth and fame in the theatre are in a distinct minority. Most actors are obliged to make enormous sacrifices to work in the profession. Is it worth the sacrifice? What are the advantages? Why become an actor at all?

We will answer some of these questions as we go along, but let's begin where every actor begins, that is, the moment you were bitten by the theatre bug and encountered the pleasures and terrors of being on a stage. A lot of us had this experience in elementary school, when we were asked to stand up and recite a poem, or in summer camp, when coerced into a play. How can you forget the first time you dressed up and pretended to be someone else? How can you forget, having finally memorized your assigned scene or speech or song, facing your first audience and seeing their faces gleam with expectation while you trembled with fear and blurted out your lines? And how can you ever forget that first delicious burst of applause?

Let's take a moment to consider that applause. Many actors recall the sound of people clapping as the event that determined the course of their lives. The notion that something you did before an audience, even as a child, could elicit such an audible expression of gratitude is bound to invade your consciousness and make you feel important in an entirely new way. Your parents may tell you every day of your life that you're wonderful. But for many years to come you will try to recapture that doting view before audiences of strangers. Applause is an experience that has become part of your destiny.

Yes, there is vanity involved in following the theatrical profession. A lot of it. But what is wrong with seeking approval and endorsement through your own professional achievements? Is that any less commendable than acquiring power, wealth, and influence in the corporate world? Admittedly, your major objective may be your own personal satisfactions, but the arts are among the few places where you can achieve satisfaction by giving others pleasure as well.

Everyone has a different memory of his or her first moment on stage. My first acting experience was the result of being unable, at the age of five, to pronounce the letter *l*. My parents, worried about a child who "ricked a rorrypop" and "ried down to go to sleep," made me take lessons designed to overcome my lazy *l*. These were offered at an institution known as "Elocution School" (I called it "Erocution School"). What my innocent parents didn't know was that Elocution School was actually a drama school for kids, the stage being in such disrepute in those days that drama teachers had to disguise children's theatre as a form of speech therapy.

After a lot of drilling in rote phrases such as "the lion leaped over the long lagoon," I eventually managed to solve my *l* problem. But at the same time that I was improving my elocution, I was performing roles in plays. The warm reception I received for these performances, even from my parents, who would have been horrified to think their child could ever consider an actor's life, were my first realization that certain kinds of work were also species of play. This—along with the pleasure of the stage and the visceral thrill of the applause—may be the reason a drama is the only art form called both a work and a play.

3

The Pleasures of Imitation

Another early avenue to the acting profession is the desire to be another person, a realization that generally occurs after watching others. It is a natural impulse and happens when you admire something so much that you want to imitate it. Through imitation, we acquire language, learn how to walk, and recognize the world around us. That is why the most basic acting exercises are based on pretending to be something else—a prowling animal or a stationary clock, a growling lion or a whirring hair dryer.

Most actors born in the twentieth century first learned to imitate movie stars. But for centuries before that, young people were attracted to a theatre career because they worshipped the stage idols of the day—Richard Burbage and Will Kempe in Shakespeare's time; David Garrick and Mrs. Siddons in the eighteenth century; Edmund Kean and Edwin Booth in the first half of the nineteenth century; Eleanora Duse and Sarah Bernhardt in the late nineteenth century; John Barrymore and the Lunts in the early twentieth.

Barrymore, for example, with his aquiline profile and emphatic snort, initiated a whole cottage industry of heroic acting in the 1920s and 1930s (Fredric March, Ian Keith, and John Carradine all owed him something), especially after triumphing as Hamlet on Broadway and in the West End. As a young actor, my idols were Laurence Olivier and Robert Newton, especially after I saw them respectively as Henry Plantagenet and Ancient Pistol in the 1944 English movie version of *Henry V.* It was the first time I realized that Shakespearean verse, rather than simply being words designed for rote memorization in high school English classes, came out of the mouths of real people. Every role I performed for a decade after would be flavored either with the clipped nasality of Olivier or the flamboyant eye-popping of Newton. I then discovered that although imitation may be the sincerest form of flattery, it is the least original form of acting.

After Marlon Brando broke into the American consciousness as Stanley Kowalski in both the stage and movie versions of Tennessee Williams's *A Streetcar Named Desire*, virtually every male wannabe actor in America was mumbling his vowels, seething with proletarian rage, glowering and walking around town, regardless of the weather, in torn tee shirts. You can see Brando's influence on Paul Newman, Steve McQueen, Jack Nicholson, Robert De Niro, James Dean, and Ben Gazzara; and even on young actors such as Joaquin Phoenix, Sam Rockwell, and Josh Hartnett today.

Hamlet calls actors "the abstracts and brief chronicles of the time," a phrase that perfectly captures their capacity to embody and reflect the style of an entire period. Some actors even have the potential to *change* the style of an entire period; this was quintessentially true not only of the young Brando, but also of the young James Dean, and today, to a lesser extent, of Tom Cruise, Sean Penn, and Johnny Depp. When Christopher Walken played Caligula at Yale in the early 1970s, scores of undergraduates in New Haven began imitating his loping walk, his eccentric speech, even the clothes he wore.

While widely copied, performers have always been considered unconventional in style and moral behavior. They can mesmerize adoring audiences while scandalizing politicians and moralists, not to mention their mothers and fathers. Remember the outrage that greeted Janet Jackson when she exhibited her breast at a football game on national television? Think of it! Exposing little children to such profanation—as if an exposed female breast were not the very first object a newborn sees. But this ability to concurrently draw down admiration and dismay is central to the performer's appeal.

"Don't put your daughter on the stage, Mrs. Worthington," Noel Coward writes in a well-known musical admonition. I would guess that many of you have experienced some of the parental disapproval suggested in that satiric lyric, even though social resistance to a theatrical career has diminished somewhat during the past fifty years. Economics are still part of the problem. An actor's career is a crapshoot, and the odds are long that you will turn up a seven or an eleven on the very first throw. Parents have feared their children will be dependent on them beyond their teen-age years, and few consider life in the theatre to be either a good investment or moral choice.

Actors don't keep the same schedules as normal people. They sleep late and stay up late, turn night into day and day into night. Although they work extremely hard when they are employed, they are often out of work, and a Puritan society considers idleness the devil's stepchild. Even in an age of relative sexual permissiveness, actors, women in particular, are still considered promiscuous, attitudes that stem from the days when the only females allowed on stage were orange girls and prostitutes.

Based on the behavior of a handful of habitual users, actors are also considered notorious addicts. John Barrymore made a career out of his weakness for John Barleycorn. So did W. C. Fields, who always carried a bottle of gin, disguised as a bottle of grapefruit juice, in his rucksack (inspiring his priceless remark, "Who put this grapefruit juice in my grapefruit juice?"). More recently, another epic boozer, Elaine Stritch, created a one-woman show about how she overcame her addiction to alcohol, and that splendid actor Robert Downey Jr. has been in and out of rehabilitation centers for years. And just as Barrymore, an incomparable Shakespearean on stage, was always best at playing alcoholics in the movies, so Stritch can be a terrific stage drunk (not so long ago in a Broadway revival of Edward Albee's *A Delicate Balance*); and Downey is unequalled in capturing the lonely despair of the hopeless cocaine addict (as he did in the movie *Less Than Zero*).

Because of their celebrity, actors are obliged to lead their private lives in public, and this is why the mistakes of the few are often seen as the misdeeds of the many. Still, there is probably some truth to the charge that actors are more likely to be less abstemious than ordinary mortals. When you're coming off the tense excitement of a taxing performance, the last thing you want after the curtain falls is to drink a glass of water and go to bed. The local bar is the modern equivalent of the Mermaid Tavern, where Will Shakespeare and Richard Burbage often traded stories (and girlfriends) over a round of drinks. (That particular establishment was located on Clink Street, and its famous brawls could explain why the term *clink* became a synonym for the hoosegow). On the other hand, the more bibulous actors of my acquaintance often struggle valorously to control their habits, realizing, no doubt, that immoderate behavior will eventually affect their performances on stage. And the great majority of actors are as balanced and healthy as anybody in the audience.

This question of moderation, dear Actor, is also related to the issue of stamina. You need a lot of strength to survive the pressures of the profession, and you shouldn't even consider acting unless you have the capacity to endure its heartaches and disappointments. For a long time, I have been convinced that one of the most important criteria for theatrical success is the capacity to stay the course, no matter how discouraging things get. I have known actors loaded with talent who did not have the will to endure rejection and disillusionment; and I have known far less gifted actors who have succeeded as a result of pure stubbornness and pluck.

My observations suggest that those who are too sensitive often lose out to those blessed with bigger calluses on their souls. There is some truth to that. But don't underestimate your capacities for overcoming adversity. Just as Chekhov was always exhorting his brother Alexander to get some iron in his blood, so I would advise you, dear Actor, if you're truly serious about being a professional actor, not to drop out because your skin is too thin. Rather, try to stick to your central purpose and, in doing so, learn how to bear the rejections and rebuffs that come your way.

Your best model in literature is Nina in Chekhov's *The Sea Gull.* Nina suffered poverty and disappointment and self-doubt, but she finally came to know that endurance is what counts:

> *In our kind of work, whether we're actors or writers, the important thing is not fame or glory, not what I used to dream about, but learning how to endure. . . . If I have faith it doesn't hurt so much, and when I think of my calling I'm no longer afraid of life.*

Remember that speech, dear young Actor, for those words will see you through.

4

An Actor's Calling

Chekhov's Nina refers to her "calling" rather than to her "profession" or her "job." What does she mean by this word? She has simply recognized that to be an actor is tantamount to becoming part of something larger than herself. We rarely use terms such as "calling" much any more; they sound suspiciously like the language employed by monks and nuns, of anchorites who mortify the flesh with scourges and hair shirts. In an age of celebrity, we are much more accustomed to seeing the fashion defer to individuals than to watching individuals subordinate themselves to a consuming purpose.

Yet, not many years ago, Ibsen was writing a lot of plays about the importance of a calling because he believed, as did Kierkegaard, that "he who forfeits his calling, forfeits his right to life."

Indeed, the corpus of modern drama is remarkable for how many plays deal directly with the tension between the private individual and the public mission, between selfishness and the selfless calling. This may be why the actor has become such an iconic figure of our time. Nobody exemplifies more prominently this particular split in the human soul between inner-direction and other-direction; nobody represents better the wide range of options available to every human being.

And nobody is a more accurate reflection of a given time. The actor is like a mirror into which everyone desires to gaze. If you achieve a really phenomenal success, your performances will be carefully scrutinized on and off the stage or screen. Actors, especially star actors, now serve the same function for us as the Olympian gods served for the Ancient Greeks; and, like debased versions of Homer, gossip columnists and tabloids record the myths of the powerful and legendary. Zeus's amorous escapades with Leda or with Alcmena, for example, have morphed into the imbroglios of Ben Affleck and Jennifer Lopez or into accounts of Madonna's various affairs and religious conversions; and in the same manner, Mary Astor's diaries once exposed to the world her various dalliances with actors and writers. Marriages, divorces, adulteries, births, and deaths involving Hollywood celebrities receive the same banner headlines as wars, revolutions, earthquakes, and famines. And if a star runs afoul of the law, as Robert Blake and Michael Jackson have, then the journalistic heavens open and pour down black rain.

This burden is a lot for one person to handle, and many an actor has wilted under the strain. The late great Marlon Brando, who had grown so elephantine that he could only be photographed if he was obscured in shadows and half light, was clearly someone whose distaste for his own celebrity had resulted in a pathological eating problem. This disorder was no doubt linked to his cavalier attitude towards acting. He famously refused to memorize his lines, preferring to take long pauses while his eyes wandered lazily towards the cue cards. He talked about his profession as if it were a mug's game (his autobiography, *Songs My Mother Taught Me*, would have been better titled *Why I Hate Acting*). Instead of graciously accepting the Academy Award he won for *The Godfather*, for example, he sent a Native American to the podium to reject the Oscar statuette in protest against Hollywood's failure to treat Indians with respect. Richard Gere accepted his Academy Award on behalf of the Dalai Lama of Tibet. Others, glancing towards heaven, thank dead parents or God, or those living surrogates for God and parents, their agents. Few manage to give the impression that the art of acting itself can be a significant source of gratitude and pride.

If you look at the way actors embrace their calling in England, you will see that something is seriously missing here in the American acting scene. It is true that respect for the actor is much higher in England than in America (and I am not counting our movie stars, who attract more idolization than respect). In England, one can become a knight or even, as Laurence Olivier did, a peer of the realm, after a lifetime of distinguished theatrical achievement. In our country, the highest public distinction an actor can receive is a presidential medal at the Kennedy Center in Washington, D.C., and that award is usually made on a condition of political loyalty to the current administration.

Still, even in England, actors can sometimes feel contempt for their profession. There is a poignant moment in John Osborne and Anthony Creighton's *Epitaph for George Dillon* during which the title character remembers when he was in the Royal Air Force during World War II, and one of his mates asked him his profession:

> *"Actor," I said. The moment I uttered that word, machine-gun fire and bombs [falling] all around us, the name of my calling, my whole reason for existence—it sounded so hopelessly trivial and unimportant, so divorced from living, and the real world, that all I could feel was shame.*

This kind of shame is no doubt shared by many actors uncertain about their profession, and that may be a reason why some Academy Award winners like to make acceptance speeches about their social and political commitments rather just thank the Academy. Deep down, they must believe that acting is an art so "hopelessly trivial and unimportant," or "so stupid, so ridiculous, so false" that it is divorced from the real world.

But as soon as an actor starts thinking of the profession as "the business," then it is inevitable that he or she will be more preoccupied with material rewards than with artistic satisfactions. Most people don't have that choice. Most professions are oriented either towards service or towards profit. In acting, the options are blurred. Many doctors, more interested in their stock investments than in the latest medical discoveries, may prefer studying *Investors Weekly* to reading *Lancet.* But their first obligation is still to heal their patients, or at least "to do no harm." Priests, ministers, and rabbis are sometimes worldly and ambitious, but their accountability is first to their God and their congregations. By contrast, some businessmen may be extremely philanthropic and some lawyers may do a lot of pro bono work, but they are in professions where the name of the game is profit. Actors are about the only ones who can choose between monk and plutocrat, maverick and mogul; who can go around in either sneakers and Levis or Armani suits and Tiffany jewelry.

So if one of the career options before you leads only to artistic fulfillment and spiritual satisfaction, another only to mass approval and material gain, you can hardly be blamed for choosing the latter. Everyone—your parents, your peers, your friends, your agent—will say you're a fool not to take the highest-paying offer, even if that sometimes means what Shakespeare called "a waste of spirit in an expense of shame."

The question remains not so much how you can pay your respects to God and Mammon both, but how you can pursue your career without losing dignity and self-respect. It is not going to be easy. In the unlikely event you do become a star, the public will believe it owns you. Your private life will become raw material for scandal magazines, your public outings meat for camcorders and digital cameras. You won't be able to go to a rest room without being followed, and although that may please your vanity at first, it will soon become a torment. Every star takes his life in his hands the moment he ventures out in public to be greeted by "adoring" fans.

But in contrast with the incivility often displayed towards actors, there are also expressions of genuine gratitude for what they bring into people's lives. Let me tell you what Stella Adler once wrote after seeing the YRT company perform Shakespeare's *Troilus and Cressida*. First, she praised the cast "for their total sense of giving us all they had—all their richness and spirit."

She went on: "And by the time they lined up to bow, I understood there is no more noble man in the world than the actor."

The nobility Stella Adler speaks about is not always evident in the sometimes tawdry world of the performer. The long rides by bus or train or plane; the sometimes dreary stopovers; the all-night restaurants and one-night cheap hotels; the peeling dressing rooms with their unemptied wastebaskets. Chekhov's Nina speaks of these trials in *The Sea Gull*, and O'Neill's James Tyrone's relentless touring schedule is one of the reasons his wife, Mary, became a drug addict. On the other hand, there is no question that, at his or her best, the actor is the vessel through which we witness the most extraordinary things of which humans are capable, whether heroic or villainous. These qualities are often embodied in the characters they play—Orestes, Jocasta, Medea, Lear, Brutus, Iago, Macbeth, Hamlet, Coriolanus, Mirabel and Millamant, Willy Loman, Blanche Dubois—people who murder and create, marry and procreate, conquer and suffer, decline and fall, rise and transcend. That preeminently human quality is also evident in the courage the actor displays just by getting up on stage. Supported only by talent he bares the inner torments of the character, and, inevitably, something of the actor's soul as well.

Many actors fear, however, that in assuming so many identities they may lose, or not even develop, one of their own. This is the dilemma of Luigi Pirandello's actor-heroine in his play *To Find Oneself (Trovarsi)*. Seeking her essential but elusive personality, she discovers that it lies not in her self but in her art, in the various roles she has played. An actor lives before a mirror and absorbs the numerous reflections being thrown back. The theatrical disguises Pirandello's heroine assumes in front of an audience are what constitute her real identity. "It is true only that one must create oneself, create! And only then does one find oneself," the play tells us. In short, the very act of creation becomes a noble act of rebellion against existence. Actors are superior precisely because they know they use disguises. They are not only the sum of their own actions, they are also the sum of the roles they play.

So do put your daughter on the stage, Mrs. Worthington. She may not always make a decent living there, but she will be part of an ancient and honorable mystery, and it is on the stage that she will most likely be able to find herself.

5

The Anti-Theatrical Prejudice

The late Shakespearean scholar Jonas Barish once wrote a book aptly called *The Anti-Theatrical Prejudice*, a history of the intolerant way in which the stage has been regarded since the earliest times. Dear Actor, prepare to meet and perhaps suffer this prejudice many times in your career. The earliest expression of the syndrome can perhaps be found in Plato's *Republic*, when the philosopher expresses his distaste for "imitation." If a chair is not as "real" as the *idea* of a chair, then the pictorial or histrionic representation of a chair is two degrees removed from reality. And so it is with poets, playwrights, and actors, all of whom Plato would banish from his ideal republic as "liars."

Their association with fakery, sham, and pretense may be a reason why actors, like the stage itself, have usually flourished on the fringes of society. Elizabethan theatres, for example, though extremely popular, were banished to the South Side of the Thames. Actors were identified by law as "Rogues and Vagabonds," and for centuries not even allowed decent burial in Christian graveyards. The Puritans sniffed that the theatre was a cesspool of iniquity (they were particularly incensed about boys playing women's parts, an act of transvestitism expressly forbidden in *Deuteronomy*). One of the first things the Roundheads did upon achieving power in England in 1642, after cutting off the head of Charles I, was to close all the theatres. Even after the Restoration of the Stuarts to the throne in 1660, Puritans such as Jeremy Collier were inveighing against *The Immorality and Profaneness of the Stage*. You can still hear the sound of those disapproving voices today.

Indeed, this distaste for imitation, if not for immorality, pervades the halls of academe, particularly in the humanities, where many professors believe that dramatic literature is better understood in the study than on the stage. But although some professors prefer to hear the play in their heads, no dramatic work can be fully realized until it is produced on stage and wrapped in the fleshly clothes of corporeal actors. William Shakespeare himself seemed totally indifferent about whether his plays were published or read (he included no more than a handful of stage directions in the acting texts). For Shakespeare, publication was something more appropriate for his sonnets. He had been dead for several years before two of his fellow actors, John Heminge and Henry Condell, collected all his works into publishable form in the First Folio.

Many academicians, on the other hand, would prefer not to see the work of playwrights they admire staled upon the stage. The stage being common and vulgar, the classroom and the library are more appropriate places for studying great works. That Shakespeare was the son of a glove maker and never went to college has led to the recent growth of Shakespeare Authorship Denial, that cottage industry of the over-educated who believe that creative genius is bestowed only on scholars holding a Ph.D. or on members of the peerage.

The distinguished Yale scholar, Harold Bloom, is not among those who question Shakespeare's authorship. But Bloom has often expressed the conviction that the best Shakespeare productions are the ones that remain unacted. "I am so weary of badly directed Shakespeare," he once moaned in typical Bloomsian despair, "that I would rather attend public readings than performances of the plays, if only such readings were available."

I once suggested publicly, only half in jest, that Bloom was not only our leading Shakespearean critic but perhaps a very good actor as well. His melancholy air, his mournful heavily-lidded eyes, and his exquisite gloom, coupled with a certain rabbinical authority, made him ideal casting for all those roles that Charles Laughton and Zero Mostel were no longer around to play, chief among them Sir John Falstaff. Although Bloom pretended to dismiss this idea, he actually became quite intrigued by it.

A few years later, when the director Karin Coonrod wanted to give a public reading of *The Henriad* (she called it *The Falstaffiad*) with Bloom in the part of Falstaff, I jumped at the chance to produce it at the American Repertory Theatre. The reading featured many members of our company, including me as Pistol. And Bloom did a rendering of the part that evoked its tragic dimension as resonantly as any Falstaff I had seen. The experience evaporated his prejudice and converted him to the theatre. Since then, he has toured his Falstaff to

New York and elsewhere, and joined the company of actors.

Theatrical prejudice is not limited to scholars. The *New Yorker*'s excellent movie critic, David Denby, once wrote an article called "Theaterophobia," the very title signifying a profound distaste for the stage. In a tour of Broadway theatres over a period of a few months, he concluded that theatre was a monumental waste of time. (It is significant that he never went to off-Broadway or to a resident theatre.)

But who can blame him or anyone else for turning off the theatre? For one thing, it can be a very uncomfortable place to sit, too airless or overly air-conditioned, with too little leg room and no space for your arms. The amount you pay for a couple of Broadway tickets might be more profitably spent on a couple of shares of IBM. Play-going can be an insufferable bore where, at times, you feel as if you were trapped in a wind tunnel with no hope of egress. Even the worst movie sometimes seems more tolerable than a bad play, because movies at least leave you alone with your fantasies. And if you want to leave, no one is watching.

So one can understand how the anti-theatrical prejudice evolves. It is up you, dear Actor, and all our colleagues in the profession, to create the kind of experiences that will wipe it away.

II.

Getting There

6

How to Act in College

All right, dear Actor, let's assume you've reached college age. How do you satisfy your passion for acting? I would warmly recommend four rigorous years of undergraduate study in the liberal arts before you enter the profession. Instead of leaping blindly and hopefully into a theatrical career at the tender age of seventeen or eighteen, first give yourself a good education in the humanities.

Today, a lot of young people skip the entire education and training process and plunge directly into show business. Some may decide to drop out of school after a year or two, as Jane Fonda did after her freshman year at Vassar in 1957, and start making the rounds. I was Jane's instructor at the time and nothing I said could persuade her to take her finals in the event she might want to return.

I still believe that Jane Fonda, good as she is, would have been a much more accomplished actor, capable of a much greater variety of roles, had she finished college. So will you. So was Jodie Foster at Yale, Natalie Portman at Harvard, and Brooke Shields at Princeton. The American theatre needs educated actors, and the more you can buttress your performing activities with humanistic knowledge the more fulfilling your future actor's life will be. You will probably want to major in theatre if your school offers such a concentration (some don't). But that is not essential. Even if you choose to pursue a BA in drama, or a BFA in a professional program such as that offered by Carnegie Mellon or Boston University, I strongly urge you to study other subjects as well, and to balance your professional classes with courses in dramatic literature.

There are many practical reasons for this. One is that you will not be in a position to understand the scripts you are sent, or investigate the role you may be offered, if you do not have some knowledge of the world in which the play takes place. You will need some background in literature, philosophy, economics, history, politics, the natural sciences, and the social sciences—the basic foundation of a liberal arts education. Most high schools these days are not very good about introducing you to the world in which you live.

As important, colleges and universities remain one of the few places in America where art survives in one form or another, be it through campus theatre, orchestras, singing choruses, museums, and visiting ballet companies. If you jump willy-nilly into the agent and audition process without giving yourself a good liberal arts education and a certain amount of exposure to the performing arts, you will limit your qualifications to approach a role intelligently. So if you are truly serious about becoming an actor in college, you will be better off reading texts instead of acting manuals.

As far as acting itself is concerned, most solid institutions of learning have excellent drama clubs, open not just to drama majors but to every student interested in theatre. Some of these are the Harvard-Radcliffe Drama Club and the Hasty Pudding at Harvard, the Dramat at Yale, the Mask and Wig at the University of Pennsylvania, the University Players and the Triangle Club at Princeton, the King's Crown Shakespeare Troupe at Columbia, and the Masquers at Amherst. The HRDC alone has attracted such fine performers as Jack Lemmon, Tommy Lee Jones, John Lithgow, Stockard Channing, and, more recently, Elizabeth Shue and Matt Damon.

And at Yale or Harvard or the University of California at San Diego, or any university that houses a resident professional theatre for that matter, somebody is likely to keep an eye peeled for undergraduate talent. The world-renowned opera and theatre director, Peter Sellars, staged his first professional production at the American Repertory Theatre while still a senior at Harvard. Ben Evett, who was a member of our company for more than a decade, was still an undergraduate when he first played on the ART stage (in the world premiere of *Big River*); he then went on to train at the ART Institute and became the theatre's leading juvenile. The multitalented Remo Airaldi, among our most versatile character actors, worked in a variety of positions at the ART during his undergraduate days—at the reception desk, in the box office, and as personal assistant both to the managing director, Rob Orchard, and to me—moonlighting on the stage of the ART until he became a fully-fledged and virtually indispensable member of the resident company. And Amy Brenneman (of the television series *Judging Amy*) was an undergraduate when she made her professional debut in the part of Juliet in the ART's *Measure for Measure*.

Whether or not you have an opportunity to appear on a professional stage during your four undergraduate years, you should try to spend your summers interning with a professional theatre group, or with a summer stock company, or perhaps at a theatre camp. The Stanislavsky Summer School at Harvard has a growing reputation. Excellent summer programs can be found at such places as the Williamstown Theatre Festival and the Oregon Shakespeare Festival, where you can pick up a lot of pointers just by sitting around the green room or by hanging out backstage with the actors. Dozens of summer theatres look for interns, particularly on the Cape: the Provincetown Playhouse, the Vineyard Playhouse, the Cape Playhouse, and the Wellfleet Harbor Actors Theatre.

As for summer camps, Camp Broadway, which trains young people aged from ten to seventeen in voice and movement and even goes on a short tour at the end of the summer, is good for pre-college aspirants. So is Stage Door Manor in the Catskills. And Camp Quisisana, on Lake Kezar in western Maine, provides opportunities for more advanced musical theatre actors to perform at night before paying guests in operas and musicals while working as waiters or maids or maintenance workers during the day.

Don't expect your summers to be paid for (except perhaps at Quisisana). At Williamstown, for example, theatre interns normally have to provide a hefty tuition as well as room and board. But you will never forget those balmy days spent building sets or assisting the director or holding a spear, for they are times of warm fellowship and shared satisfactions.

7

The Case for Advanced Training

Once you have emerged from the cloistered precincts of your university, dear Actor, what next? What about advanced theatre training? Should you apply for full-time study at a drama school, or should you take classes in the various acting studios while making the rounds? Should you undertake formal training in your chosen profession, or should you move to New York or Los Angeles, find a job waiting on tables or temping in an office, and hope for the best? Should you spend a few more years in a protected environment, or should you pray for an agent while poring over *Backstage* for audition possibilities?

For me, this is a no-brainer. I believe, if you can afford the hefty fees, there is no sensible alternative to advanced professional theatre training. Few people make it on talent and instinct alone. As the melancholy saying goes, you can't find an agent without a job, and you can't find a job without an agent. Indeed, the odds against finding regular work without representation are depressingly high, especially if you have not yet gained your acting legs. I have seen the children of too many friends move from home and scavenge the city, lonely, depressed, and disappointed, to believe that anyone is going to succeed on blind luck and without proper training.

It is true that Richard Burbage did not go to drama school, or even to college, and neither did Edmund Kean or Sarah Siddons. Indeed, few great actors in the past had a higher education (some didn't even go to high school). But they were often self-taught, and they had the brains and the will to do a lot of reading. Having discovered their metier at an early age, these actors were never deflected from pursuing it.

But actors then had a training ground, one that is now largely obsolete: I am referring to the various stock companies that toured every region in the land. It was in such venues that young Elizabethan actors first learned their craft, that Molière evolved as an actor and a playwright, that David Garrick and Edmund Kean dazzled a rural public. It was there that young people took apprenticeships, watched seasoned performers from the wings, sat in the green room and picked up theatre lore, and occasionally went on stage as an understudy. My late friend Fredric March, one of the leading actors of the American stage and screen (he was the original James Tyrone in the premiere performance of Eugene O'Neill's *Long Day's Journey into Night*), always boasted that he had never spent an hour of his life training to be an actor. He learned from getting up on stage and doing it. So, by the way, did O'Neill's father, James O'Neill (the model for March's character in *Long Day's Journey*), who toured as a lad with Edwin Booth, who claimed to have read every play ever written, and who "studied Shakespeare as you'd study the Bible."

Until Constantin Stanislavsky and Vladimir Nemirovich-Danchenko inaugurated the Moscow Art Theatre in 1898, in fact, there were no acting schools to speak of. All the training was done on the job. Before Stanislavsky, there had been a few published theories of acting (Denis Diderot's eighteenth-century *Paradox of Acting*, for example, which described the difference between emotionalism and antiemotionalism, and François Delsarte's nineteenth-century *System of Oratory* with its stylized codes of expression and gesture). But Stanislavsky's great accomplishment was to translate the instinctual approach of the great actors he had seen and worked with into a codified method of "realistic" acting. In short, he was able to systematize what was natural and inspired into a technique that could be emulated through reading and practice. When the Moscow Art Theatre first visited our shores in 1924, American theatre people were so dazzled by the actors Stanislavsky had trained that in 1931 some of them inaugurated an art theatre of their own. It was called the Group Theater, the first company to come out of a training process, and it produced the finest actors in the land.

Using the principles Stanislavsky discussed in his various books—especially *An Actor Prepares*—his American followers first set up summer classes for their acting company, then hired a Broadway theatre for the purpose of putting on a succession of new plays. This intimate link between training and performance would remain constant throughout the Group Theater's existence and serve as a model for future repertory companies. Unfortunately, the Group ran out of money after nine years, and its actors were lured away to Hollywood.

Following the demise of the Group Theater, many of its alumni, having lost their theatre, became master teachers and passed on their versions of the Stanislavsky system to others. The most celebrated of these was Lee Strasberg, who took over the Actors Studio two years after it had been established by Harold Clurman, Elia Kazan, and Cheryl Crawford in 1947. But the Actors Studio was only one of several acting laboratories, some of which still exist, that were created by such legends of the Group Theater as Bobby Lewis, Sandy Meisner, and, preeminently, Stella Adler, the only member of the Group who had actually met Stanislavsky and who bitterly disputed what she felt to be Strasberg's corruption of the Russian master's method.

Some of America's most famous actors were trained in these studios. Paul Newman, Marilyn Monroe, Kim Stanley, Geraldine Page, Ben Gazzara, Ellen Burstyn, and others joined the Actors Studio (James Dean spent a few weeks there as well). Marlon Brando and Robert De Niro became Stella Adler's students. Robert Duvall and Joanne Woodward took classes with Sandy Meisner. Indeed, training became so enshrined that it was sometimes considered more important than performing. One reason for this was the absence, after the Group Theater died, of a genuine art theatre in New York. As mass entertainment eclipsed serious drama and musicals replaced the straight play as the dominant form of Broadway, the acting studio became virtually the only place where actors could continue to believe that they were serious artists working in a respectable profession. (That may be why the name of an acting manual by another great actor and acting teacher, Uta Hagen, is called *Respect for Acting*.) It was in the acting studio—and not on Broadway—that they were able to perform scenes from great plays by Anton Chekhov, Henrik Ibsen, Samuel Beckett, and Eugene O'Neill. It was there they could continue to believe that what they were doing was important.

In the 1960s, acting training underwent a major revolution with the development of intensive programs connected to universities. The Yale Drama School had been a major player in this arena since the late 1920s, along with Carnegie Mellon (earlier known as Carnegie Tech). When I signed on as dean at Yale in 1966, one of my first decisions was to create a professional repertory theatre that would at the same time serve as a model for the students, as a place for them to apprentice, and as a permanent home for those qualified to join the company after graduation. In the future, these young people would provide the new talent and fresh energies of the American theatre.

This idea of a university-based professional theatre-*cum*-acting school was later to be adopted at Brown University (in association with the Trinity Repertory Company), at Harvard (in association with the American Repertory Theatre), at the University of Chicago (in association with the Court Theatre), at the University of California at San Diego (in association with the La Jolla Playhouse), at the University of Minnesota (in association with the Guthrie), and, in modified form, at Princeton (in association with the McCarter Theatre).

Whether or not theatre programs are affiliated with professional theatres, you can choose from a host that are connected to academic institutions: NYU's Tisch School; Columbia's School of the Arts; Berkeley, UCSD, and most other branches of the University of California; the North Carolina School of the Arts; and many more. Other good training centers, such as the California

School of the Arts (founded by Disney), and the American Conservatory Theatre, have no university affiliation. New York's Juilliard, which began as a conservatory of music and dance, later added an excellent theatre school and now offers a BFA degree in acting. This program was created in 1969 by the great teacher-director Michel St. Denis, who founded the Old Vic Theatre School, and it was later led by John Houseman, an associate of the Federal Theater who had also founded the Mercury Theatre with Orson Welles.

If you want to specialize in a particular method, however, say that of Tadashi Suzuki, you would be better off studying with a single specialist teacher such as Anne Bogart, who teaches the Suzuki-influenced Viewpoints method in New York and (during the summer) in Saratoga Springs. If you want to study the Method, then you should go to the Actors Studio school and train with the disciples of Lee Strasberg. But if you want a more comprehensive training that will expose you to every conceivable form of playwriting from Aeschylus to Tony Kushner, you would be better off attending a traditional drama school or conservatory.

So there are numerous places in the country available to those who wish to engage in serious acting training. Each will have a somewhat different focus and approach, which may change with each change in leadership. The Tisch School, for example, once had a history of training for such experimental ensembles as the Performance Group, Mabou Mines, and the Wooster Group, especially when Richard Schechner was its reigning guru. Now it has broadened its program under the direction of Zelda Fichandler, the founding artistic director of the Arena Stage, and one of the godmothers of the resident theatre movement. As for Yale and Harvard, these drama schools are also inclined to develop actors for the resident theatre movement. With enough research, you will undoubtedly be able to identify the institution that will best help you develop the skills you need for your chosen profession.

Just make sure that you apply to more than one.

It is always sensible to hedge your bets. You will probably be asked to accompany your application with a transcript, a statement of purpose, and written endorsements from your undergraduate teachers and others who know you personally. In the old days, that was enough. Students at Yale were admitted on the basis of good grades and academic recommendations (as I was). Today, you will be required to audition—more important than the highest grades or the warmest letters.

Audition requirements vary from school to school, but usually applicants are asked to prepare a classical and a modern scene, each between three and five minutes long. Select scenes that play to your strengths. If you have a gift for transformation, don't be afraid to choose a character role. If you don't yet have a talent for characterization, choose something closer to your own age and personality. Most people on the selection committee, however, want to see variety, so make sure your two scenes are sufficiently distinct from each other to impress your auditioner. You may also be asked to improvise and sing a song, even if it's only "Happy Birthday." And don't be afraid to be funny. After listening for days on end to scene after scene, often the same ones, auditioners are grateful for a laugh.

8

How to Act in Drama School

As I don't know which acting school you've chosen, the models I am going to talk to you about are the ones I know best—the Yale School of Drama and the ART Institute for Advanced Theatre Training at Harvard. Yale's is a three-year program leading to an MFA degree; the ART Institute is a two-and-a-half-year program leading both to a certificate and an MFA. There is no denying that, by going to these schools, you are going to incur a costly debt. Scholarships are available, but they are rarely enough to cover your entire tuition and living expenses. You will be living on loans, and whatever supplements your parents can afford to give you. Your love of acting will be tested early because you will be paying off these loans for most of your young life. It is one of the burdens of your profession that training for it is so dreadfully underfunded.

It is also true that places in these programs are extremely limited—Yale admits about twenty-two actors each year, Harvard about eighteen. I also realize that, for geographical, financial, or personal reasons, you may want to attend an entirely different school. But Yale and Harvard are typical enough of other acting programs to serve as examples. And both institutions have been sufficiently effective in turning out successful actors to enjoy credibility as training centers.

These conservatories, as I have previously mentioned, are associated with professional theatres, their major advantage being that they offer acting students the opportunity to work with seasoned actors. Some of these actors will be your mentors not only on stage but in the classroom as well, because many of them (in the Stanislavsky tradition imported by the Group Theater) not only act but teach. The prototype is the traditional guild model of master and apprentice. The older actor mentors the younger in an ancient craft which, ideally, is then passed on to a third generation when the student is advanced enough to become an actor-teacher as well.

In the Harvard program, you will have the added advantage of three months in Russia at the Moscow Art Theatre School during the spring of your first year (your first summer in Cambridge will include intensive instruction in the Russian language). This period will include not only training in acting but also the opportunity to develop a production under the supervision of a Russian director, such as Romon Kozak or Alexander Marin, that will be shown to the public in Moscow and later in Cambridge. But the greatest advantage of this period abroad is the opportunity to spend time among passionate theatergoers in a city where the theatre is considered an essential activity of everyday life. Institute students return from this experience virtually transformed inside and out, having absorbed a lot of the Russian spirit and aesthetic.

The director of the Moscow Art Theatre School is the world-renowned theatre scholar Anatoly Smeliansky, author of definitive books on Mikhail Bulgakov, Vladimir Stanislavsky, and the Moscow Art Theatre. Indeed, Tolya, as he is affectionately called, spends a few months each summer and fall in Cambridge, along with a substantial number of Russian teachers in acting, directing, and movement. As a matter of fact, your MFA degree will be awarded by the Moscow Art Theatre School, and not by Harvard, which will give you a certificate in drama.

Yale and Harvard developed their training techniques to provide artists for the flourishing resident theatre movement in America. And it was those theatres—some of them extinct pioneers, such as Andre Gregory's Theatre of Living Arts in Philadelphia; some of them still flourishing, such as the Guthrie Theater in Minneapolis, the Trinity Rep in Providence, the Alley Theatre in Houston, the American Conservatory Theatre in San Francisco, the Chicago Shakespeare Theater, and the Shakespeare Theatre in Washington, D.C.—that determined the aesthetic and rationale behind the various training programs.

The best kind of program, therefore, is not one that features a master acting teacher, but rather one that makes the resident theatre itself the master teacher. I won't go as far as David Mamet in saying that most master teachers are frauds. But a lot of them certainly limit the kind of styles and approaches that an actor can study. Making the theatre itself the master teacher can train students for all the kinds of plays produced by the theatre, however. At Yale and Harvard, the playwrights we most admired were Chekhov, Shakespeare, and Brecht, so our training was organized around the styles associated with their plays. We proceeded, therefore, to use

Stanislavsky as a basic building block, because his technique continues to be the most effective way to initiate acting training. But Stanislavsky was only to be a foundation stone, not the whole building. The diversity of American theatre required a much more eclectic form of architecture.

Stanislavsky, as the founder of what is known as modern realistic acting, and the director most intimately connected with Chekhov (a sea gull still remains the logo of the Moscow Art Theatre he founded), dominates the first year's training at both Yale and Harvard. At Yale when I was dean, and at Harvard presently, the first year was devoted to "poetic realism," with Chekhov as the model of the form and Stanislavsky as the model of the theory informing it. Acting students are taught about "objectives," "actions," and "intentions" in their studio work, and they perform exercises in "given circumstances." They also explore the issue of the "subtext," or the meaning that lies beneath the lines, which may often be the very opposite of what is being said. Voice and movement are essentially remedial and corrective; they are designed to hammer out speech defects and physical awkwardness and include instruction in phonetics, voice placement, fencing, and acrobatics. A script breakdown course revolving around such plays as *Ghosts*, *The Father*, and *The Cherry Orchard* introduces students to modern realism from the actor's point of view.

At Yale, the final project of the first year was always a play from the "poetic realism" canon—*Three Sisters*, say, or *A Doll's House*—staged by one of the directing teachers; and the play was cast in a way that gave every actor a chance to play against type, and it was performed two or three times before a school audience. Meanwhile, the first-year actors at both schools were obliged to undertake small responsibilities with the professional company—walk-ons and minor roles—so they could have some contact with the Rep without scanting the obligations of their class work.

Although the ART training is more compressed, the second year of this sequence at Yale was devoted to verse training, Shakespeare functioning as the model playwright. Having absorbed the Stanislavsky technique, with its devotion to truthful acting based on the examination of personal experience, students could now go on to apply these techniques to classical drama. Voice classes were devoted to scansion and verse speaking; singing classes consisted of madrigals and Elizabethan airs by Dowland and his contemporaries; movement was period dancing and stage combat—the core techniques for performing in verse plays, whether Greek or Renaissance. A mask class complemented the acting classes, geared to improvisations based on characters from commedia dell'arte or Shakespeare clowns, that used to culminate in a rowdy, obscene cabaret presentation supervised by Jeremy Geidt. And the final project was a poetic drama by one of the great Elizabethan or Jacobean playwrights—Marlowe, Jonson, Middleton, Ford, or Tourneur. As for the second year's relationship to the Rep, they were asked to understudy featured roles, and, to motivate these assignments more seriously, each student had the opportunity to play his or her understudy assignment at least once before a matinee audience.

In their final year, the acting students at Yale, as at the ART, were prepared to play important roles at the Rep (though, if qualified, they might even play such roles in an earlier year). As younger members of the company, final-year students would have more obligations to the Rep than to the school, so they had fewer classes and more rehearsal hours. Nevertheless, the class work—in what we called "postmodernism" (Luigi Pirandello and after)—was concentrated and intense. Voice work included singing, primarily the songs Kurt Weill wrote for Bertolt Brecht's lyrics, and movement courses introduced the students to Aikido, a nonviolent form of Japanese combat. Script breakdown concentrated on the plays of Brecht, Pirandello, Beckett, Handke, Shepard, and other postmodernists; and the final acting project was designed to be a highly experimental free-form exercise directed by a visiting acting teacher—say, Lee Breuer of Mabou Mines, who took his Yale class through a fascinating shadowgraph version of *Earth Spirit* (the basis for his notorious *Lulu* at the ART in 1980), or Andrei Serban, who directed his class in a version of Shepard's *Mad Dog Blues* performed on the beach at West Haven. As if these students did not have enough to do, they were also expected to form a cabaret company and perform skits, songs, and satires at Yale Cabaret when they managed to find a few idle hours.

The purpose of this three-tiered program was to develop a versatile transforming actor. I am thoroughly convinced that an actor trained in these three major styles is capable of performing in almost any play ever written, and in any medium.

Thus, both the Yale and the ART programs accept the preeminence of the Stanislavsky technique as a training method, but not as an exclusive procedure, part of a trajectory that aspired toward the classical literature and experimental drama from a platform of truth, honesty, and imagination. And the various script breakdown courses are designed to ensure that the student is familiar with the entire literature of the field so that not only are his or her special talents brought to the profession but also sufficient general knowledge and cultural background.

It is crucial that you, as an actor, know the literature of your profession. Nothing irritates a director more than to offer someone a role in Shakespeare, Chekhov, or Tennessee Williams only to hear the response, "I don't know the play—send me a copy of the script." Sometimes expressing ignorance about a text is a canny way of stalling on a decision while waiting for a better offer. But it also suggests that many American actors—perhaps the majority—do not know very much about their own field. Imagine if Itzhak Perlman, having been asked to perform the Brahms Violin Concerto with the New York Philharmonic, said to the conductor, "Let me read the score first." Why are musicians so much more familiar with the literature of their field than actors?

So a good training program will usually try to shape both your mind and your body, your intellect and your emotions. The relationship between classroom work and practical stage experience should always be the keystone of any training curriculum. One cannot exist without the other. Yet, there will always be tensions between the two approaches. Both the acting teacher and the acting student have to be sensitive to the need of establishing the best possible balance. That balance is what will make you the completely fulfilled and well-rounded actor you aspire to be.

9

Into the "Real World"

After two to three years in the relatively protected, if often competitive atmosphere of a drama school, you will now find yourself trembling over the prospect of being thrust into what some actors refer to as the "real world." These last months in training are generally the most highly pressured and anxiety-ridden of your time in drama school. Aside from portending the breakup of a close-knit community, they represent the end of a learning process and the beginning of a preoccupation with career. You will start thinking less about parts in plays than about your glossy photographs and résumés, and more about how to sell yourself than how to develop your talent. No surprise. You are probably very heavy into student loans and they have to be paid off so that you don't end up in debtor's prison.

Acting programs often contribute to this anxiety by concentrating the efforts of the final few months not so much on training and development as on what is generally known as the "showcase." Showcase. The very word suggests that your eye will no longer be on process but rather on the result: on perfecting the scenes you are going to display to people positioned to help with your future employment.

I recognize the necessity of the showcase, but I wish it were not the climactic moment, and possibly the last memory, of your drama school years. Nothing is more likely to confuse that experience with what is scornfully called "vocational" training. Graduate students in medicine, law, business, and education, for example, are of course obliged to interview for jobs, but rarely are they asked to "showcase" for them. On the other hand, actors are the only professionals whose only instrument is themselves. Opera singers have their voices, musicians have their clarinets and violins, artists have their paints and palettes and easels. What you've got is you. Artistic directors, producers, and agents are unlikely to travel very far to see you in a play, therefore it is your melancholy obligation to bring yourself, a moveable feast, to them. This presentation usually takes place in New York and Los Angeles, often in coordination with the presentations of other drama schools. You choose the scenes under the supervision of your acting teacher.

The major question is how to present yourself. You will probably have the opportunity to showcase two five-minute scenes, generally with another actor, and you may have a chance to sing a song. The conventional wisdom these days is that potential employers in New York and Los Angeles are only interested in your value as a commercial commodity, so you'd better choose your material from among lightweight Broadway comedies and musicals, forgettable movies, or television sit-coms, and your song from the latest Tony-award-winning musical. It saddens me that actors who have trained for years in the great plays of world literature should be judged when they complete that training on the basis of inferior material. If that is what the commercial world wants to buy, then I suppose you have to sell it. Driven by fashion and convenience, most people in casting are looking for clones of what is already popular and established rather than for something fresh and original. These clones are known as "types" ("Get me a Brad Pitt type" or "Get me another Catherine Zeta-Jones"). Indeed, there is a cruel joke about the short life of actors in Hollywood that is based on how casting agents typically describe the progress of an aspiring star. First they ask "Who is John Doe?" then "Get me John Doe!" then "Get me a John Doe type!" and finally "Who is John Doe?" (The alternate joke about fading careers is "Keir Dullea, gone tomorrow.")

But I have yet to be convinced that a smart agent would not respond more enthusiastically to an actor who makes a strong showing as Benedict or Beatrice in *Much Ado*, or as Oswald reaching for the sun in *Ghosts*, or as Nina saying farewell to Treplev in *The Sea Gull*, than to someone who tries to counterfeit the urban antics of characters from "Sex and the City," or any other momentarily fashionable "types."

Remember, too, that you have additional avenues to employment apart from casting agents who are unfamiliar with your work, or from actors' agents who are interested only in saleable commodities. If your drama school admits in theatre disciplines other than acting, then your fellow students could be invaluable future resources when you're looking for employment. Students trained in directing, in administration, and even in dramaturgy may be in a strong position to help you after you all graduate. The directors, being personally familiar with your acting from the time you spent together as students, would be more inclined to cast you in their productions, or to recommend you to other directors; the administrators to hire you when they find jobs as managing directors with theatre companies or as producers of films; and the dramaturgs might even end up evaluating your performances if and when they find jobs as critics (there is, of course, no guarantee those reviews will be positive). The network you set up in drama school—at Yale this was known as "The Web"—can be an invaluable resource to you throughout your professional life. I speak from personal experience. I got a lot of work during my freelance acting days, both in television and theatre, from friends I knew in drama school.

In addition to contacting friends, do not hesitate to write to the artistic directors of theatres where you would like to act. Make certain you are familiar with the work of that theatre, and do not be reluctant to express your admiration. (All artistic directors, including me, are vulnerable to flattery.) If you are truly eager to be associated with a company, express your willingness to commit for an extended period. Some artistic directors are so demoralized by the constant defections of their acting company to television or the movies that their antennae are highly tuned to someone who promises to be constant and loyal to a not-for-profit theatre.

I remember receiving a letter followed by a phone call, when she was still a very young woman, from Pamela Gien, the South African actress who later made such a strong impression as the author and actor of *The Syringa Tree*. I was so flattered by her passion for the kind of work we did, and so touched by her despair about finding another place to do it, that I immediately invited her to audition. She stayed with our company for three seasons, leaving only when her husband's job pulled her away to California.

Plan very carefully. Your appeals and your demeanor could earn you an interview, an audition, and a job.

10

When Worlds Collide

This brings us to the next important question, dear Actor, namely, the kind of choices you will be forced to make upon leaving your drama school. And perhaps the most persistent one will test the tension between your obligations to your career and your obligations to your art. Take a deep breath on that one. It is a conflict that will dog you for the rest of your life.

Stanislavsky put it best: “Love the art in yourselves rather than yourselves in art,” he advised his actors. What did he mean by that beautifully balanced aphorism? Well, first of all, Stanislavsky was urging young people to purge themselves of egotism, a fault that is occasionally known to afflict a few in our profession. He was saying that self-love and vanity do not properly serve the arts, and, in fact, may well be an obstacle to genuine self-investigation.

He was also saying, however, that talent is a gift of grace, that it must be nurtured and tended, like a beautiful garden. And he was saying that, because it doesn’t belong to you alone, it must never be used for base purposes. "I have been a poor caretaker of my talent," wrote the novelist F. Scott Fitzgerald, regretting how much precious energy he had squandered in the pursuit of pleasure and the consumption of alcohol. He knew that it was his obligation to preserve the gift he had been given, to make certain that it was being used for the highest possible purpose.

Yes, you could answer, it is easy for you to make such high-minded declarations. You have some cash in your checking account and a regular income, including some of the money I spilled for your book. But how am I supposed to get rid of my student loans, keep up with my rent, and pay off my credit card debt while caretaking my talent and loving the art in myself?

You are asking a fair question; indeed, it is one that has caused me considerable anguish in recent years when I have tried to counsel acting students. It was easy enough to talk about moral choices during the years when the not-for-profit theatre movement was flourishing, and actors were finding regular employment in resident companies. These theatres were prepared to provide a living wage to actors on seasonal contracts—admittedly, not a windfall, but enough on which to live and even raise a family.

But then came the assault on the National Endowment for the Arts (a Puritan backlash against sex and blasphemy in the Mapplethorpe and Serrano affairs), which drastically reduced federal subsidies to not-for-profit theatres—at the same time that most private foundations were developing interests other than the arts. (Later, the entire economy would begin to tank, affecting individual philanthropy as well.) The result of these cutbacks was a severe reduction in the number of companies offering regular work to actors. Today, there are no more than twelve resident acting companies left in the League of Resident Theatres, a not-for-profit service organization that includes more than two hundred institutions, and most of these hire only a handful of actors on seasonal contracts. (I'm not counting the large Shakespeare companies, such as the excellent Chicago Shakespeare Theatre, or the Oregon Shakespeare Festival, which operates primarily in the summer).

So how can I exhort you to consider a career in the not-for-profit theatre, or even the commercial theatre, when the opportunities are so limited and the pickings so slim? How can I counsel you to choose the stage over film or television, both of which promise so much money if you succeed in breaking through the charmed circle?

Well, in all conscience, I cannot. It is the nature of our system, and a consequence of the current crisis in the arts, that you will be pulled inexorably into the marketplace, whether you like it or not (and a lot of you will wonder what's not to like, considering the rewards). I am perfectly aware that most of your acting activity will take place in areas other than the theatre and that, if you have a choice, you are not going to waste a lot of time waiting on tables or addressing envelopes in the slim hope of being cast in a play. From a practical point of view, and simply as a strategy for survival, you must take the most lucrative work that is offered to you, and hope against hope that this will be in circumstances that will not corrupt or abuse your talents.

On the other hand, I am also impractical enough to believe that what attracted you to acting in the first place was a desire to play the great roles in company with like-minded people, and, whether consciously or not, that you want to continue your artistic development throughout your life. For that reason, a lot of my advice is going to be long-range and idealistic rather than short-term and expedient; my assumption is that the problems afflicting American theatre at the moment are not permanent, that the time will come again when our culture will be in a position to help you flower as an artist.

In short, although I shall continue to give you practical tips that I hope you will find useful in the short run, I will also try to remind you of the values that underlie the ideal theatre, whether you care about these at the moment or not. I hope you will forgive me for pestering you on this score. It is my experience that most good actors pester themselves about it a lot more.

11

Looking for Work

All right, let's say you are walking the streets of New York (Los Angeles, Chicago, Houston, San Francisco, Boston), looking for work. You are astonished by the price of apartments, you are unwilling to settle for the flea-bitten studios in Astoria or Crown Heights, and you are not ready to lower your rent payments by advertising for roommates you do not even know. You are hamstrung by not having a job or an agent who can help you find a job. Let's assume that your showcase has appealed to an agency that will agree to negotiate for you if you do get an offer and that you are now hanging around Equity headquarters looking for casting opportunities. You do not want to ask your parents for any more financial support. You are more than a little depressed. What should you do?

Read, go to museums, go to shows, and get a job.

The job may be part-time or full-time, but it will at least liberate you from the need to depend on your parents or scarce acting opportunities for financial support.

And it will enable you to be a little more choosy about the parts you accept, assuming that parts are being offered. Your greatest consolation will be to identify classmates or friends in the theatre who are willing to get together of an evening and read plays. It is not impossible that this reading group will turn into a small company, and if you rent a loft for a few nights, you may even have yourself a theatre. Any number of small effective companies started this way—Mabou Mines, the Wooster Group, Steppenwolf, Cornerstone, the Aquila Theatre Company, the Performance Group, Greasy Joan, Red Bull—and with some decent luck, yours might have some staying power, too. You will not make a living in this manner, but having the chance to speak a few lines of dialogue can still be a great consolation. Your need to remain active and productive while you work at a job that probably does not fulfill you will be partially satisfied.

This transition period from drama school to a job in the theatre has the potential to be the most demoralizing time of your life. Do not be discouraged. Everyone goes through it. Some actors decide at this point to abandon the profession. I confess that I did, long, long ago in a distant galaxy, after I took a year off from the teaching that was providing my livelihood and allowing me to "make the rounds." It was not that I did not find work. I was given acting jobs fairly regularly in Equity Library productions, television specials (through the help of classmate directors), and commercials. It was just that I found the work—and the process—too demeaning. The parts I was being asked to audition for were of such low quality that, in my youthful arrogance, I decided the theatre was not worth my time, especially as I had little respect for the people who were judging my talent. I chose to go back into academic life.

I was lucky. I had an option. And I could continue to pursue my love of theatre by acting and directing in various college drama departments. I was also developing a knack for writing about the stage that allowed me, as a critic and theatre commentator, to see a lot of contemporary productions.

But my summers were what really saved me, for this was when I could find work with companies I admired and perform in plays I respected, often in lovely bucolic settings. Three of these companies I helped to found. The first was Studio 7 in New York's Greenwich Village, where we performed in an off-Broadway postage-stamp house called the Provincetown Playhouse. The second, called Group 20, was in Unionville, Connecticut, where we lived in the mildewed cellar of an abandoned bank and performed in the local town hall. And the third, after this non-Equity group turned professional and moved to Wellesley, Massachusetts, came to be known as Theatre on the Green, which produced a goodly selection of the classical repertory, giving me the chance to do my Laurence Olivier and Robert Newton impersonations in such roles as Bottom the Weaver and the melancholy Jaques. Those performances, presented outdoors in dew-drenched, star-dazzled nights, were the best theatre experiences of my life.

To be sure, these were part-time activities. Chekhov called literature his mistress and medicine his wife. Henceforth, I would be married to academia. If Kingman Brewster, Yale's president, had not invited me to serve as dean of the Yale Drama School, thus reviving my dormant appetite for the practical stage, I would probably still be teaching at Columbia and writing full-time drama criticism for the *New Republic.* In my defection from the theatre, I had failed a crucial artistic obligation for an actor, which is to be tenacious, stubborn, persistent, undaunted. If you truly want a life in the theatre, do not make that mistake yourself.

III.

Being There

12

Some Exemplary Careers

Perhaps the best way I can exhort you to keep your connection to the stage is to talk about the careers of a few American actors. Some, I helped train; others, I worked with in my various theatres. Each actor faced the same dilemmas that you will confront, though their options were no doubt somewhat wider when the resident theatre movement was in full flower.

Let's start with Meryl Streep, one of the most celebrated actresses in contemporary America. The arc of her career is an illustration of how a smart and well-trained actor can continue to exercise control over her career right through middle age. Meryl came to the Yale Drama School in 1972 from Vassar College, where she had the opportunity not only to play leading roles in the Vassar Experimental Theatre but also to study under such literary taskmasters as Evert Sprinchorn (a leading authority on Ibsen and Strindberg) and Leon Katz (a brilliant analyst of Samuel Beckett and Gertrude Stein). Meryl's native intelligence was probably as keen as that of any acting candidate in American history. But it certainly helped that, in addition to her opportunities for performing at Vassar, she was exposed to some first-rate scholars in dramatic literature.

When Meryl arrived at the Yale Drama School, it was immediately apparent that she was destined for greatness. I first met her at a reception for entering students during the fall of her first year, and I was powerfully struck by her insinuating beauty and lively mind. I remember thinking that she would be the ideal actor to play the temptress Lulu in Wedekind's *Earth Spirit*, though it was a part she never got the chance to act. Instead, she made a tremendous impact in her second year at Yale as the "ancient translatrix" Constance Garnett (the bane of every graduate school as the clumsy translator of Chekhov, Dostoyevsky, and Tolstoy) in a student spoof on Russian literature called *The Idiots Karamazov*. The authors were Christopher Durang and Albert Inaurato, both of whom would later make their marks in the American theatre—Durang with such plays as *The Marriage of Bette and Boo* and *Sister Mary Ignatius Explains It All for You*, Inaurato with *Gemini* and *The Transfiguration of Benno Blimpie*. Streep would take her first steps into theatre history in her role as Constance Garnett.

You young actors who may be contemplating cosmetic surgery in the belief that physical beauty is the key to stardom should know that Meryl played the part of Constance Garnett in a wheelchair; she had a huge mole on her gigantic putty nose, and her eyes oozed plumtree gum. An American beauty of the first degree, she had the courage to disguise her good looks under tons of makeup so that she could realize the full dimensions of her part. Her wheelchair was pushed around the stage by an actor impersonating Ernest Hemingway, whom she hectored mercilessly. By the end of the play, she had transformed into Miss Havisham (the ancient doyenne of Dickens's *Great Expectations*) and concluded the evening by irritably waving her cane at the audience and shouting "Go Home! Go home!"

It was a stunning performance, but the kind that would normally be expected to repel agents and alienate casting directors. For Meryl, it immediately established her as an actor of the highest order. I was so dazzled by this student performance that I rescheduled the play in the 1973–1974 Repertory Theatre season. It followed another Dostoyevsky-related work, *The Possessed*, in a production staged by the great Polish director Andzej Wajda. Indeed, Wajda himself was so impressed by Streep that he cast her in *The Possessed* as well, opposite Christopher Lloyd, so that in the same season, she was performing both in a Russian play and in a satire on Russian plays.

It took no particular skill or acumen to know that Meryl was the real thing, and, as a result, I made her the leading lady of our professional company while she was still in her third year at the Yale Drama School. That decision created a lot of envy and some resentment among her classmates. She not only played the two roles mentioned above but, in lightning succession, a neurotic analyst in Charles Dizenzo's *The Shaft of Love*, Bertha in Strindberg's *The Father*, and Helena in Alvin Epstein's exquisite production of *A Midsummer Night's Dream*, which supplemented the text with the complete score of Purcell's *The Faerie Queene*. As if this were not enough, she played a bit part in and understudied the leading role of Lillian Holiday in *Happy End*, with its gorgeous Brecht–Weill songs.

And further, she also played that part for three performances, with only two hours notice, when the other actress became sick. (She reprised the part a few years later in New York opposite Christopher Lloyd as Bill Cracker.)

We were working this enormously gifted actress very hard, and as a result her commitment to her studio work suffered. Her acting teacher, the Group Theater actor and director Bobby Lewis, who had also cast her that year as the lead in a student production of Sean O'Casey's *Cockadoodle Dandy*, began complaining that she was not showing up for his classes. As dean, I had to arbitrate between her growth as a professional actress and her obligation to her class work, not an easy task when it was I who was overloading her schedule with professional assignments.

Meryl asked to be excused from the last production of the year, the Shakespeare/Purcell *A Midsummer Night's Dream.* I could not bear the thought of losing her in the rôle of Helena, so I suggested that we let her understudy replace her in the Strindberg. This idea, which seemed reasonable to me, struck Meryl as disastrous. The problem was that Rip Torn was playing the title role of *The Father*, Method-style. He had entered the part of this psychopathic figure so completely that he tended to treat Elzbieta Chezevska, the actress playing his wife, so roughly on stage that he left bruises all over her body. "He really thinks I am his daughter," Meryl said, adding that, no matter what we told Torn about an understudy in the part, he would stop the show upon her entrance and shout, "Where's Bertha?"

As a result, despite her exhaustion, she agreed to play both Helena and Bertha if we would excuse her during that period from Bobby Lewis's classes. I agreed, thus relieving the excessive pressure on Meryl at the cost of disgruntling Bobby. By the time she graduated, in 1975, she was the toast of New Haven, and an extremely appealing prospect for New York producers and directors.

Despite all my efforts to keep her in New Haven as our leading lady, she took off for New York: "To try my wings," she explained in a letter to me. "The Rep is home . . . and you've given me opportunities and encouragement that form the basis of my confidence in and commitment to the theatre." But she never returned "home." She was cast almost immediately in productions at the Phoenix Theatre and at the Public Theater, under the legendary Joseph Papp. When Papp took over the Lincoln Center Theatre Company, she was chosen to play an elastic-limbed Dunyasha in Andrei Serban's critically acclaimed production of *The Cherry Orchard*, with Irene Worth. Soon she was tapped for Hollywood, where she won her many Oscar nominations (the first along with another of our company alumni, Christopher Walken, in *The Deer Hunter*), and entered the pantheon of great American actresses.

Meryl's success in Hollywood has been distinguished and continuous even into her middle age because she was trained as a character actress and not as a star. Her capacity to gravitate between comedy and tragedy, between glamour queens and ancient biddies, has been the quality that distinguishes her from so many actors with shorter careers. It hasn't hurt, either, that she was able to establish a stable family life: Her devoted husband is the sculptor Don Gummer, and she is the mother of four gifted children.

Meryl's career is one that young aspiring actors would do well to emulate. It is true that she did not return to the stage as often as I hoped, or as she promised in her letter, largely for family reasons. When she did—as Madame Arkadina, for example, in Mike Nichol's Shakespeare in the Park production of Chekhov's *The Sea Gull*—she exhibited all her old spunk, passion, and comic flair. (The three stage roles she played, also under Nichols's direction, in the HBO version of Tony Kushner's *Angels in America*—Mother Pitt, Rabbi Chemelwitz, and Ethel Rosenberg—further demonstrated her infinite variety). Meryl Streep is one of those American actors who bring honor to her profession—serious, dedicated, versatile, and, above all, as smart as they come.

Another career I would like to praise is that of Mark Linn-Baker. I have known Mark ever since he was an undergraduate at Yale College in the mid-1970s. The first time I saw him perform was in a Feydeau farce produced by the undergraduate Yale Dramat, where he stunned me with his grace and agility. He had the goofy charm of a young Buster Keaton, the choreographic nimbleness of a young Charlie Chaplin, and the antic clownishness of a young Emmett Kelley. Clearly, this young man was destined for something in the theatre, but was he a serious actor?

Bobby Lewis, then head of the acting department, did not think so. After Mark had auditioned for the Yale Drama School, I asked for the young actor's folder; I expected to read "Accepted" on the cover, but I saw that he had been rejected. "An undergraduate actor," Bobby said dismissively. "Take him!" I snapped imperiously. I was not accustomed to overruling the acting department on its applicants, but I had seen enough of this young man during his undergraduate performing days to believe that he was the real thing. True, he was not yet a finished performer, and he had not yet demonstrated that he could play a dramatic part. But I was not going to let the acting department lose this inspired comic to another drama school.

Mark's career at the Drama School was impressive. Like Henry Winkler, who had gone through the program earlier, he was everyone's choice for comic roles (Henry was particularly good at playing clowns in children's shows). In our 1978 Yale Repertory Theatre production of Brecht's *Man Is Man*, Mark, playing an assistant Bonze (or Buddhist priest), practically stole the show with his only line: "It's raining."

He became one of the founding members of the ART company when we moved to Harvard in 1980, opening in a revival of Epstein's now legendary *Midsummer Night's Dream.* This was the same production that had featured Meryl Streep as Helena in 1975. Now some five years later, all the student parts and most of the professional parts had been recast, and Mark was in the role of Puck, reprising one of our greatest successes in front of Cambridge audiences.

It was as if the part had been written for him. His sprightliness, his impishness, his sly grin and his high intelligence were all perfectly suited to the character of this Shakespearean mischief maker who causes so much confusion among the Athenian lovers. He had demonstrated his artful agility the previous year during our 1978 tour to Cambridge in Andrei Serban's production of Molière's *Sganarelle* as the "flying doctor," a character who pretended to be two people on stage at the same time. With the aid of some extraordinary calisthenics, Mark actually persuaded the audience that he was two people on stage at the same time.

Mark's Puck, the opening shot of the new company in its quarters at the Loeb Drama Center, was the first in a series of splendid performances he contributed to the company and to the community. Mark's final performance of that year was as Khlestakov in Gogol's *The Inspector General*, Peter Sellars's first professional production. Mark more than held his own against a spectacularly postmodern approach to the play in which this delightful impostor took his departure by flying over the audience.

Although Mark would return to the ART in future years to act in a few shows (and to direct a play by Christopher Durang), this was effectively his last production as a regular company member. Like Meryl before him, he was eager to try his wings in New York. It was hard to let him go. I had envisioned Mark growing past the juvenile roles he was playing, going on to the big ones—Iago, perhaps, or even Hamlet—and finally, as befits the status of senior actor, playing older characters and mentoring the young.

It was not to be. Mark was quickly picked up for a few movies, and then for a television series called *Perfect Strangers*, just as Henry Winkler had been snatched away years earlier to play the Fonz in *Happy Days*. For both of them, their work on camera resulted in a kind of runaway media success that ended their theatre careers for a while.

It was not just contractual demands that kept these good actors from returning to the stage; it was their popular identification with one character. Henry Winkler, for example, though a nice Jewish boy from Long Island, impersonated the Fonz, a charming Italian goofball clone of Stanley Kowalski, with such effectiveness that his fans could not separate him from his role. Returning to Yale one day to talk to the drama students, Henry was the picture of melancholy in the midst of success. People, he claimed, were simply unwilling to separate him from his television persona. His situation reminded me of the clown in a Marcel Marceau skit: He puts a grinning mask on his face and then, to growing consternation under his grin, cannot pull it off. Mark's Larry in *Perfect Strangers* did not quite have the same popular appeal as Henry's Fonz, but it put similar handcuffs on his theatre career.

Mark well understood that no matter how lucrative or celebrifying his television career became, the real satisfactions of an actor were to be found in theatre. And he vowed that however successful he became in other media, he would never abandon the stage. As a matter of fact, he went on to co-found a company of his own—the New York Stage and Film Company—partially dedicated to the production of new plays.

Let me cite another exemplary career suspended between stage and screen, that of Tony Shalhoub. Tony was a 1980 graduate of the Yale Drama School (Mark was class of 1979), where he soon displayed such a powerful and idiosyncratic talent that I invited him to join the ART company the day he graduated. Tony's initial appearance at the ART was as the First Fairy, buried under a ton of green greasepaint, in still another revival of *A Midsummer Night's Dream.* But he was soon shuttling between Beamarchais's Figaro, Molière's Valère, Chekhov's Solyony, Angelo in *Measure for Measure*, Joseph Surface in Jonathan Miller's dark version of Sheridan's *School for Scandal*, Pozzo in Beckett's *Waiting for Godot*, and the Son in my own production of *Six Characters in Search of an Author.* In five seasons, he graduated from juveniles to character roles, from lovers to heavies, a transforming actor of the first rank.

In the mid-1980s, Tony left the company—yes, to try his wings—and worked in movies and television series (including *Wings*), where he often found himself—typed by his Lebanese features—impersonating Arab terrorists (in *Men in Black*, he played an alien pawnbroker with huge ears and an elastic face). On the other hand, he returned to the company as often as he could between gigs. He performed in the occasional new Mamet play (*The Old Neighborhood* opposite his wife, Brooke Adams), and, most notably, played the title role in Diderot's *Rameau's Nephew*, in which he displayed a wit of such ferocity that he electrified the house. The only time he disappointed me was when I offered him the role of a lifetime in Ron Daniels's production of *Hamlet*, and he turned it down. (The part was quickly snapped up and played brilliantly by Mark Rylance, who went on to lead the Globe Theatre in London). To his credit, Tony did not use the customary actor's delay, "Let me read it first." He knew the part intimately. But his agent had told him that there was a series pending and he could not pass up what seemed to be a great commercial opportunity.

Tony Shalhoub is such a loving, warmhearted, and good-natured individual, and so loyal to the ART, that I soon recovered from my disappointment, though I still tease him for having thrown away an opportunity that most actors would kill for. Eventually, he found a television part that was worthy of his remarkable powers of transformation when he was cast in the title role in *Monk*, the neurotic, hypochondriacal detective who manages to solve mysteries in spite of serious mental and physical handicaps.

Speaking of transformation, let me cite another versatile actor of the Yale class of 1980 who joined the company upon graduation and who has remained with us to this very day, namely Thomas Derrah. His may not be a name you recognize; indeed, he has steadfastly refused celebrity and chosen instead to develop the art in himself. I would not have predicted that Tommy was destined for the not-for-profit theatre. In his youth, he had the quality of a young Mickey Rooney, blessed as he was with a high comic energy, a fabulous sense of movement, and a gorgeous tenor voice that any musical comedy star would kill for. I thought Tommy was headed for Broadway musicals, and I imagined I was going to spend a lot of time trying to talk him onto the serious stage.

I was wrong. Tommy needed no coaxing. He was always a theatre artist from the top of his shiny head to the tips of his nimble toes. His first role at the Rep was Puck, replacing Mark Linn-Baker, in a revived version of *A Midsummer Night's Dream* that we moved to the Wilbur Theatre in the fall of 1980. When Tommy was asked to play Sganarelle in a revival of *The Flying Doctor*, he grumbled that he was always being treated as a stand-in for Mark.

Tommy was, he believed, capable of much more than comedy roles, and he proved to be right, though his greatest triumph, I believe, was in a raucous musical version of Jarry's *Ubu Roi* called *Ubu Rock* where he played a one-eyed, one-armed general and sang a monotonous patter song that never seemed to end. This provoked the audience into throwing programs and coats at him in mock frustration (Tommy threw them back). Over the next twenty-four years, his roles were as varied as Uncle Vanya and Charlie Chaplin and Shlemiel the First, and culminated in a controversial characterization of Richard II as a flaming queen. Not only had Tommy established himself as the quintessential repertory theatre actor, praised by critics, admired by audiences, beloved by fellow company members, he had become an expert teacher and director in his own right. Of all the young people I have helped to train, Thomas Derrah may be the one who best exemplifies the values of the ideal theatre—selfless, dedicated, hardworking, and not reluctant to sacrifice material rewards for the sake of a continuously developing art.

Another actor who joined us in *Midsummer* (playing a bored Hippolyta), and who has remained with the ART to this day is Karen Macdonald. A Boston-born performer trained in cabaret and improvisational theatre, Karen, like Tommy Derrah, was an instinctive musical comedy virtuoso, equally adept at singing and dancing, and she had an instinctive gift for farce. What was most satisfying for me was to see her develop into a fine serious actress. Perhaps her greatest performance to date has been in Brecht's *Mother Courage*, as staged by the Hungarian director Janos Szasz. She interpreted the title character as a wretched woman who gradually loses everything she loves to war and her own greed; in the final scene, she hauls a train of baby carriages round and round the stage in blank despair. Today, Karen functions as one of the backbones of our company in plays as far afield as the Greeks and Pinter, alternating between comedy and tragedy, character women and leading ladies: a universal actress.

Still another fine example of a stage-dedicated actor—indeed, today many consider her the first lady of the American stage—is Cherry Jones. Cherry joined our company in 1980 for the Wilbur Theatre version of *A Midsummer Night's Dream.* She played Helena, the part that helped to launch Meryl Streep. (That *Midsummer* production has obviously proven to be the springboard for a lot of remarkable careers.) A native of Tennessee, and a graduate of Carnegie Mellon, Cherry was clearly destined to have a significant acting life from the first moment she stepped on stage. Dimpled, apple-cheeked, goodnatured, intelligent, tall, and blessed "with endless legs" (as the *Newsweek* critic Jack Kroll described her), she started a lot of male hearts pumping, though for most of her career her own heart was loyally devoted to her female partner.

Cherry quickly became our leading lady and stayed in residence with the company for twelve seasons. She accompanied us on tours to Avignon, Edinburgh, Asti, Israel, and Yugoslavia, always the personification of good sense, high spirits, and liberal politics. One of Andrei Serban's favorite actresses, she contributed performances as Irina in *Three Sisters* and Viola in *Twelfth Night* that changed our perceptions of how these parts could be played. When she left the company, it was less for career reasons than out of personal loyalty. She couldn't continue to be separated from her partner, an architect living in New York. On Broadway, she won a Tony (and the admiration of audiences and critics alike) playing the lonely spinster in *The Heiress.* From there, she rarely made a false move, only accepting parts in plays she believed in. She also made occasional movies such as *Erin Brockovich* and *The Cradle Will Rock* (cast as the legendary Federal Theatre pioneer, Hallie Flanagan Davis), though Cherry's was essentially a stage face and voice, not really suited for the camera.

She returned to us from time to time, especially in a crisis when we were most in need of her—as, for example, when she instantly agreed, after we had already opened *King Lear*, to replace a sick actress in the part of Goneril, on short notice and with no expectation of reviews. We could always count on Cherry's generous presence at galas and fundraisers. And she paid me the personal compliment of returning to the ART to play and sing the title role of *Lysistrata* in my very last production as artistic director in the spring of 2002. A truly fine human being.

Another gifted and devoted ART actor is Will Lebow, born in New York. Will long ago determined that his heart was in company work, and that the city that provided him the best opportunities was Boston. Will was trained in the classics at the Boston Shakespeare Company, which he helped to found, and in comedy and improvisation (he is the Voice of Stanley in the cable television animated series *Dr. Katz, Professional Therapist*). But it took me a little time, and several auditions, before I realized that he had access to a much deeper side of his talent. Perhaps his best demonstration of this was as Shylock in Andrei Serban's 1998 production of *The Merchant of Venice.* Although Will is Jewish, he made no effort, as so many actors do, to soften the anti-Semitic aspect of the role. Indeed, he exaggerated it by playing Shylock as a Catskill burlesque comic with a Machiavellian streak who goes for the jugular whenever his financial wires are crossed.

Since then, with his expert timing and sonorous voice, Will has alternated among comic characters (Gronim Ox in *Shlemiel the First)* and leading men (Valère in Molière's *Miser*) and tragic heroes (Marat in Peter Weiss's *Marat/Sade)*, playing five or six roles a year in a manner that makes him seem like a new company actor every time he sets foot on stage. As the tragic Father in Adam Rapp's *Nocturne*, he was heartbreaking, and he performed the part of Heiner Mueller, the hapless hero of Charles Mee Jr.'s *Full Circle*, with such a mixture of wiliness and panic that he won the Elliot Norton Award for Best Actor of the Year.

A list of exemplary careers would be incomplete without Stephanie Roth-Haeberle. Stephanie first joined the ART in 1990, playing Maya in Robert Wilson's production of *When We Dead Awaken*. Her fine body structure, deep-set eyes, wide mouth, irresistible smile, and high cheekbones accounted for an extraordinary beauty. But it is the texture of her soul that makes her performances so memorable. She is one of those rare actresses who combines sweetness of temperament with depth of character.

Stephanie spent several seasons with the ART, then left to get married and have a baby. In between feedings, she became one of Woody Allen's regulars, usually in small parts. But when her child was sufficiently grown, she was able to return to the ART for one play at a time: She flexed her muscles in imitation of Arnold Schwarzenegger as the Spartan Lady Lampito in *Lysistrata*, writhed about in a lunatic asylum as a suffering, emaciated Charlotte Corday in *Marat/Sade*, and, most recently, in the Robert Woodruff *Oedipus*, she played an accessorized Jocasta as if she were a Fifth Avenue matron, drinking champagne out of her shoe, vacillating wildly between the heights of exultation and the depths of grief. She is one of the great underappreciated actors of our time.

Two more career examples and I am done—Jeremy Geidt and Alvin Epstein. Both of these splendid artists were with the YRT from its New Haven beginnings in

1966, though Alvin occasionally took a season or two off for other opportunities, including a brief tenure as artistic director of the Guthrie Theater in 1978. The first time I saw Jeremy perform was as a member of a British satirical group called *The Establishment*, a successor to *Beyond the Fringe* and a forerunner of *Monte Python.* It was obvious then that he possessed the kind of waggish wit that we associate with the best English comedy. As an actor who had taught with the legendary Michel St. Denis at the Old Vic Theatre School, Jeremy had repertory in his very blood and sinews, so it was not too difficult to persuade him to spend his life acting with our company and teaching our students. (His most popular courses were Shakespeare performance and his celebrated mask class).

"Endowed," as I once described him, "with the barrel chest of a Toby jug and the delicious vocabulary of a foul-mouthed sailor," Jeremy is a perfect example of how an actor can mature through affiliation with a secure place that benefits as much as he does from his development. Having played more than two hundred roles with the company, including a definitive Falstaff and a raucous Sir Toby Belch, he is now in semiretirement at the ART, still teaching full-time but acting on a reduced schedule.

Alvin Epstein, who trained with Marcel Marceau and Lee Strasberg—an unlikely combination—has also been one of the most valued members of the senior company, both as an actor and as a director. Making his professional debut as a mime in New York, where he held placards for Marceau, he later went on to play Lucky in the first American production of *Waiting for Godot* (with Bert Lahr, E. G. Marshall, and Kurt Kasznar) and the Fool in Orson Welles's *King Lear.* Epstein is a prime example of the virtue of intelligence, as opposed to intellectualism, in an actor. To watch him doing table work with a full cast, as a director parsing a Shakespeare play, is to be convinced that really smart actors can penetrate a text more deeply than the most erudite scholars. And to watch him on stage in the great variety of roles he has played—from the Greeks through Molière to Beckett (he and Jeremy did a symbiotic Didi and Gogo together that was a moving testimony to their long association)—is to see a consummate theatre artist in motion.

There have been only intermittent opportunities for Alvin in the commercial theatre, though his own ambitions have often led him there. I know this has been disappointing for him because, in a healthier Broadway, he would have become one of its leading figures. Alvin exemplifies the difficulties that a genuine man of the theatre experiences in a profession dominated by greedy producers, celebrity actors, and untrained audiences.

I have written about these many exemplary careers to give you some sense of the options you face upon graduating from drama school, but also to keep on encouraging you not to lose your connection to the stage. It remains the most direct link to your innermost being. Without that link you will never truly realize your potential. And to paraphrase Saint Mark, what shall it profit actors if they should gain the whole world and lose their immortal roles?

Forgive the messianic tone, but I truly believe that, under the proper circumstances, the theatre can continue to be a form of artistic salvation for you. That said, go the way you must, and do the best you can.

13

The Transforming Actor

Along with John Gielgud and others, dear Actor, I believe that all great acting is character acting. The really important actors extend themselves to the role they are playing rather than make the role conform to their own limited biographies. The Latin phrase *dramatis personae* literally means "the masks used in the drama," indicating that, from the very beginning, actors were expected to conceal their own faces with the exaggerated features of someone else. In Italian commedia dell'arte, as you may know, the characters of seventeenth-century comedy—clowns with names such as Arlechino, Brighella, Smeraldina, Pantalone, and the like—disguised their faces with masks that made their characters immediately recognizable to audiences. This made it possible for commedia actors to play these stock characters well into their old age, and to be replaced—with no loss of continuity after they died or retired—by actors wearing the same masks. It was the comic type, and not the individual actor, who contributed the performance, and the comic business, or *lazzi*, was part of a continuing tradition.

No one (except perhaps the Japanese in Noh plays and perhaps Eugene O'Neill in *The Great God Brown*) expects contemporary actors to cover their faces with masks, though some use so many false beards, fake noses, wigs, and other disguises that they might as well be wearing masks. Indeed, nose putty and face hair are the common currency of character actors. Sir Laurence Olivier, for example, used to claim that he found the key to such roles as Richard III only when he decided on the shape of his nose. (Playing Shylock, he also delighted in wearing large protruding false teeth.) But Olivier found the right nose for Richard only after he found the right models for this epic villain, a combination of a Broadway director he detested (Jed Harris) and the Big Bad Wolf. Aside from using external aids, every great actor learns how to subordinate, or at least to merge, his or her personal qualities under the characteristics of the role being played. That is another way of assuming a mask.

This method is called is working from the "outside in." Other actors work from the "inside out." As Olivier said: "The actor who starts from the outside is more likely to find himself in the parts he plays than to find the parts in himself." The interior actor, by contrast, represents the alternative tradition of realism that disdains the use of masks in the service of "truth" and "honesty." This style—for that is what it is, another style—is a very recent phenomenon on the theatre scene, dating from the mid-nineteenth century.

The fact is that every period claims to have made advances in "truth" and "honesty" over the previous age. Great actors throughout history have been acclaimed for their powerful sense of naturalness as compared with the fakery that preceded. The critic Leigh Hunt, for example, praised the "freshness" of Edmund Kean as compared with the "external and artificial" Thomas Kemble. Coleridge added the famous remark that "to see Kean was to read Shakespeare by flashes of lightning." Other contemporary critics demurred: "Kean is called a natural player," one wrote, "but his style of acting is highly artificial and technical." Another added, "I know of no more irksome noises than those which issue from his breast."

In other words, what seems authentic and convincing to one generation usually seems false and spurious to the next. Just listen to an old recording of John Barrymore reading Hamlet's "To be or not to be" or Richard III's "Now is the winter of our discontent" and you will understand how an actor praised for his extraordinary realism in the 1920s can now sound excessively hammy. Even Marlon Brando's legendary Stanley Kowalski in the film version of *A Streetcar Named Desire*, a performance that literally changed our minds about the nature of American realism, in that we could not tell the actor from the role or the role from the actor, now seems like a brilliant exercise in style. (Years later, when Brando played Vito Corleone in *The Godfather*, stuffing his cheeks with Kleenex to create the mask of old age, he demonstrated that he had been a character actor all along.)

What I am suggesting is that every actor needs some artificiality in order to achieve the illusion of reality. How else can you speak "naturally" in a large auditorium and still be heard by hundreds of people? In movies, a microphone allows interior intimacy, but up on stage you have to project. This illusion in the service of art is what Picasso meant when he referred to "lies like truth," a phrase that Harold Clurman recycled as the title of one of his books. The question is whether the truthful lie you tell is about yourself and your own personality and experience, or about a character far removed from yourself. In other words, whether you work from the outside in or the inside out.

These are hardly new debates. In the eighteenth-century, Rousseau (like Plato) scorned "imitation," so essential to an actor's art, as spurious and unoriginal. This idea later informed Stanislavsky's directives, formulated in reaction to the artificiality of "imitative" Russian acting. But not long after Stanislavsky had invented his naturalist technique, one of his followers, Vsevolod Meyerhold, invented its counter technique, a kind of supertheatricalism far removed from realism, which in turn was modified by another theatricalist approach created by another Stanislavsky actor, Yevgeny Vakhtangov.

Gordon Craig's desire to turn the actor into an "Ueber-Marionette" was a sign of his revulsion against an acting style that robbed the theatre of its size and theatricality. And Bertolt Brecht's famous "alienation techniques" were another effort to wrest the theatre (and acting) away from Stanislavsky's realistic grip and return it to the epic freedom of the Greeks and the Elizabethans. The followers of Stanislavsky seem very like the disciples of Freud in the way they have continually revised and rebelled against the master's precepts.

In our own time, Lee Strasberg modified Stanislavsky's system in a way that managed for a while to give character acting a bad name (his interior approach actually proved more appropriate to the movies, where most of his students flourished). He had obviously failed to read the next volume after Stanislavsky's *An Actor Prepares,* namely, *Building a Character.* It was Stella Adler, having gone to Paris to work with Stanislavsky in 1934, who revealed that Strasberg had corrupted the Stanislavsky system with his relentless insistence on "affective memory" and "personal" (rather than "given") circumstances. Stella reminded us that Stanislavsky wanted the actor to be fully conscious, not to invade the unconscious in the manner of a patient on a couch. Strasberg's modification of the Stanislavsky system into the "Method" had the result of creating highly neurotic actors entirely dependent on recalled material from their own psychic lives—which is one reason why Bobby Lewis called his book on the Strasberg technique *Method or Madness?*

Whatever your method (or madness), some form of disguise is not only an aid to acting but also a basic necessity when you are a member of a company. Audiences will tire of anyone who appears before them in weekly repertory without changing character from one play to another. This kind of laziness encourages the actor to take histrionic short cuts, another word for which is *mannerisms*—"those cushions of protection," as Olivier called them, "which an actor develops against his own self-consciousness." Mannerisms bore the audience and provoke the critics. If you do not explore each succeeding role from a completely different point of view, then your shelf-life as an actor is going to be very limited indeed.

Speaking of character acting, this might be the moment to bring up the very knotty issue of multiculturalism in the theatre, because it is not only a social phenomenon but an aesthetic one, an extension of whether you work from the inside out or the outside in. There has been some debate recently, to which I have added my voice, about whether actors of color should only play parts identified with their own racial or ethnic background—or whether these actors should choose and be chosen for a greater variety of roles purely on the basis of talent, an alternative that has come to be known as "nontraditional casting."

In the twentieth century, there was always controversy about whether white actors should be allowed to play characters of color. After centuries of segregated theatre, when whites were blacking up not just to perform in minstrel shows but to play black characters in classical plays, such roles are now primarily reserved for African American actors (Olivier was one of the last Caucasians with the chutzpah to play Othello in blackface). The same is true of Asian characters. In the past, studio heads could choose Peter Lorre, a German Jew, as Mr. Moto, and Warner Oland, a Swede, as Charlie Chan. But when the British actor Jonathan Pryce was cast as the Engineer, a Eurasian pimp, in the Broadway production of *Miss Saigon* in 1987, Asian actors protested Pryce's Anglo-Saxon descent.

It looked then as though one of the by-products of multiculturalism was to doom us to a future of racial type casting. I had occasion to debate the distinguished American playwright, August Wilson, on this subject some years ago. Wilson had proclaimed in a speech that black actors should perform only in plays written by black playwrights. He rejected "color-blind" or "nontraditional" casting as "the same kind of assimilation that black Americans have been rejecting for the past 380 years." Given that it was segregation, not assimilation, that characterized the American stage for 380 years, this was a melancholy thing to hear. Just at a time when black actors in the resident theatre were getting the chance to play not just Othello and Aaron the Moor but also Antony and Hamlet, just at a time when Asian actors, previously cast primarily as house boys, were performing major roles in Shakespeare, Molière and Chekhov, along comes this new separatist movement and self-segregation.

Of course, August Wilson is right in saying that black people should have their own theatre. Every American ethnic group should have its own theatre. There has certainly been no dearth of such manifestations in America—from the Yiddish and Italian theatres at the turn of the century to the Negro Ensemble Theatre and the Repertorio Espanol in more recent times. America is a diverse nation, but it shares many common values, and to restrict actors to their own racial or ethnic types is to limit them.

José Ferrer, a great Puerto Rican actor, was a superb Cyrano de Bergerac and a terrific Iago to Paul Robeson's Othello; and the black actor Canada Lee was also responsible for a superb Caliban. The best Kate I ever saw was the African American actress Jane White in the Central Park version of *The Taming of the Shrew.* And the most convincing Shlemiel in my ART production of Isaac Bashevis Singer's *Shlemiel the First* was not one of the Jews who played the part but rather our own Tommy Derrah, a Baptist from Maine. Recently Denzel Washington, Laurence Fishburne, Morgan Freeman, Andre Braugher, and countless other distinguished actors of color have been playing the great roles from the world's store of dramatic literature, and playing them with great distinction.

Limiting actors to their own racial or ethnic groups is precisely the sort of thing that the resident theatre is dedicated to changing. Like personality acting, it inhibits the full play of the creative imagination. As an actor, you must learn when to use your personal characteristics, and when to ignore them. Personality acting is only of limited interest to an audience that quickly tires of seeing the same person in the same kind of role overusing the same idiosyncracies and the same tricks.

Sigourney Weaver came to Yale determined not to be a personality actor. An uncommonly beautiful woman, she would probably have been grabbed by Hollywood regardless of her acting ability. That may be the reason she implored the acting department to cast her against type, that is, in parts that did not exploit her good looks. As a result, she was assigned several roles she would never normally play, among them Didi in an all female production of *Waiting for Godot.*

Sigourney would later complain that Yale did not sufficiently prepare her for the "real world," meaning the commercial arena that every actor eventually enters. But considering how quickly she achieved Hollywood stardom, it was not really necessary to prepare Sigourney for the "real world." Her training had made it possible for her to bridge the range of roles she played both in the movies and on stage. By following her earlier instructions and our own inclinations, Yale had helped make her into a character actor rather than just another pretty face, enhancing her powers of transformation.

14

The Actor's Intelligence

Sigourney, like her Yale classmate Meryl Streep, is an extremely smart lady, which leads me to the subject of my next letter: the actor's intelligence. An actor can benefit from a good brain, but intelligence in the acting profession does not mean a high IQ or straight A grades. Most actors correctly believe that over-intellectualizing a role can have a damaging effect on one's emotional understanding of it. If a great intellect were the mark of a great actor, then Albert Einstein would have played the Godfather instead of Marlon Brando, and Susan Sontag would have been cast in all of Judi Dench's roles.

But there are many forms of intelligence apart from the scholarly and the academic. And just as you need not be a brain surgeon to dissect an acting part, you need not be a ninny, either. Plays are peopled with characters, and the better you understand human behavior in a historical context the better prepared you will be to fulfill your part. This is not to denigrate the importance of instinct, or the intelligence of the heart ("The heart has its reasons which the reason knows not" is the way Pascal described this instinctual intelligence). But just as the brain needs an emotional component, so the emotions also have to be educated if you are going to play characters with more depth than inarticulate studs or brainless floozies.

This has been another major quarrel with the Method as it has been taught and practiced in this country: Many believe that it is a system geared too much to the personal experience, inner emotions, and natural instincts of the actor and not enough to the imagination or to the world beyond the self. There is no question that understanding a role must begin with self-understanding. But knowing the self is simply a first step towards building the truth of a character. Self-knowledge can't re-create a historical environment. It can tell you something about the psychological condition of classical characters, but not what motivated these people in relation to their political, social, and cultural surroundings. As long as Method actors are playing characters close to themselves, generally working-class Americans with explosive personalities, they can impress us with their power and believability. But the moment they step into the shoes of heroic characters from the past, they are likely to stumble and fall.

No male actor is going to discover the moral dilemmas of Hamlet or the spiritual torments of Lear in his own psychological history; nor will a female actor learn much about Lady Macbeth or Phaedra by exploring her own political ambitions or sexual desires. Because these characters live in a particular historical moment, they are endowed with responsibilities and fates of a kind unfamiliar to us moderns. How can we learn more about them? First, through the imagination, and second, through reading and research—not so much in theatre scholarship, unless this is considerably less abstruse than most writing on the drama these days, as in other plays of the period, as well as in period history, art, religion, and philosophy.

If you are to make a role your own, and not simply a historical construct or a narrow contemporary re-creation, you have to know what to use and what to reject from the past; otherwise, you may end up the butt of jokes, as John Wayne was when he played a Roman soldier at the Crucifixion in some biblical epic. Asked by the director to read a line he was drawling with a little more "awe," Wayne redrawled: "Awww, truly he is the son of God."

If I sound critical of theatre scholarship, please understand that I am not talking about commentators who can really help you understand a playwright—such as William Arrowsmith on Euripides, Harold Bloom and Stephen Greenblatt on Shakespeare, Michael Meyer on Ibsen, Evert Sprinchorn on Strindberg, Martin Esslin and Eric Bentley on Brecht, Robert Scanlan on Beckett, among many. I am advising you not to waste your time with the deconstructionists and theorists, those critical extraterrestials who spew such alien words as "semiotics" and "grammatics" and "signifiers," who would like to replace performance with "performativity," and theatre or dramatic art with "performance studies" or "performance theory." Beware of such language. It is rarely spoken by people who love the theatre.

You may not find a lot of these postmodern scholars inside drama schools, though their number and influence are growing. In some training centers you may find no scholars at all. But it is your obligation to navigate a course between the Scylla of abstruse scholarship and the Charybdis of ignorant instinctualism by choosing what is valuable for building a role and rejecting what is irrelevant.

Consult anyone who has an intelligent word to say about the play you are rehearsing, and do not hesitate to do a lot of reading on your own. If there was a dramaturgy or literary management program at your school, take advantage of the students who graduated from that program. In short, grab your help wherever you can find it.

15

Film Versus Theatre

I have been pontificating about the primacy of the theatre over the screen for actors. Why? Because the stage is where you can truly perfect your craft and sullen art. The great Swedish director Ingmar Bergman, who has worked in both forms throughout his long life, retired from directing recently with these words: "Theater is the beginning and end and actually everything, while cinema belongs to the whoring and slaughterhouse trade." Now that is a strong statement, and a surprisingly harsh one coming from a great film director. He is saying that, considering all the money riding on each film, the end product belongs to the people who provide the financial backing, and that person, with the possible exception of Mel Gibson, is rarely the actor.

Furthermore, the observation that whereas the theatre is an actor's medium, the movies are dominated by the director is now a cliché. Your very best moments on screen may end up as celluloid scrap on the cutting room floor because the director (or the director's boss, the producer) believed your scenes did not advance the story.

Instead of letting you build your character as you do in the theatre, movie directors are always asking you to start from scratch in the middle of an emotional moment. Instead of being allowed to interact with other human beings, you are required to express emotion to a mechanical piece of plastic, metal, and glass called a camera, a machine that never answers back or feeds you cues.

Instead of acting, you are submitting yourself to being photographed. And whereas in the theatre your character belongs to you alone once the show opens, in the movies your role is marginal, provisional, and cuttable. In the words of the heroine of *Stage Door*, an ode to the theatre by Edna Ferber and George S. Kaufman,

> *[Acting movies] isn't acting; that's piecework. You're not a human being, you're a thing in a vacuum. Noise shut out, human response shut out. But in the theater, when you hear that lovely sound out there . . . it's as though they'd turned on an electric current that hit you here. And that's how you learn to act.*

Of course I'm exaggerating. A lot of actors swear by film, and there have been numberless great movie performances—almost always, by the way, contributed by people originally trained for the stage. But these are actors who have learned the virtues of minimalism and the secret of how to preserve the integrity of a performance. Brando's brooding intimacy was, from the very beginning, perfect for movie roles, as was the goofy menacing smile of Robert De Niro. As a young man, Al Pacino was brilliant as Don Michael Corleone in *The Godfather* because of his instinctive sense that the secret of his character's growing depravity was not in boisterous threats or menacing behavior but rather in the quiet reasonableness of his voice and in the gradual deadening of his eyes. Some years later, when Pacino began to introduce flamboyant stage techniques into his movie performances—first in *Scarface* and later in *Heat* and *The Devil's Advocate*—a completely different actor emerged, not always a convincing one. But Pacino's outsize acting was perfectly appropriate for the theatre when he returned there to play *Richard III*, and the title role in Brecht's *Arturo Ui*, and Herod in Wilde's *Salome*.

My general point is that if you are well trained as a stage actor, you should be prepared to play in any medium. Not always. The plummy-voiced John Gielgud, unlike his fellow British knight, Laurence Olivier, never seemed totally comfortable in front of the camera, except perhaps as Dudley Moore's disdainful butler in *Arthur*. It is instructive to compare Gielgud's resonant Cassius in John Houseman's film of *Julius Caesar* with the intimate Brutus of James Mason and the hooded Antony of Marlon Brando. (Gielgud himself described these performances in his letters: "James Mason . . . talks through his nose and Marlon looks as if he is searching for a baseball bat to beat his brains with.")

Gielgud's performance is designed for the stage, Mason's and Brando's for the movies. But Laurence Olivier, Richard Burton, Ian Holm, Albert Finney, Claire Bloom, Judi Dench, Meryl Streep, Robert Duvall, Gwyneth Paltrow, Robert Duval, Edie Falco, Kevin Kline, Liev Schreiber, Elizabeth Mastrantonio, and a host of other distinguished stage-trained actors have made the leap between film and theatre with extraordinary ease.

The opposite, however, is rarely true. Movie stars without theatre training or experience very rarely make much of an impression on stage. Audiences have been forced to endure a huge number of bad celebrity performances—usually on Broadway, but not always limited to Broadway—because producers need stars to attract large audiences to their shows. Hugh Jackman, trained in the Australian theatre, commutes with ease between Hollywood's *X-Men* and Broadway's *The Boy from Oz*. But the rap artist Sean Combs never quite managed to get his tongue around Lorraine Hansberry's dialogue in *A Raisin in the Sun*, and neither Ashley Judd nor Jason Patric had the stage chops required for *Cat on a Hot Tin Roof* (Ned Beatty, their stage-trained co-star, lost a Tony nomination for saying this out loud). New York's Shakespeare in the Park often likes to buff up its image with luminaries slumming from Beverly Hills, even though this free theatre hardly wants for overflow audiences. I remember a particularly trying *Twelfth Night*, for example, starring Michelle Pfeiffer and Jeff Goldblum—two actors I much admire in the movies. Neither of them had the slightest inkling about how to play a Shakespearean role.

Admittedly, these are the kind of luminaries the public really wants to see, and in a world of crowds and anonymity, you may envy the way Hollywood stars are recognized wherever they go. But compare the appeal of fame with the advantage of being able to live, and perhaps raise a family, in the city where you work, recognized on the street by your fellow citizens not as a celebrity but as a familiar neighbor who gives them regular satisfaction on the stage.

I have yet to mention the greatest advantage of company acting in particular and the stage in general, and that is the possibility of building and participating in a genuine community. At a time when Americans find themselves divided by separate and competing interests, when our streets are dangerous and often devoid of strollers, when people are tempted to withdraw into the refuge of their living rooms and home entertainment centers, we are in real danger of mutating into moles. How many activities actually bring us out into the street? Going to church or synagogue is one. Going to the theatre is another, and when we squeeze into a theatre chair, narrow and uncomfortable though it may be, at least we are in a room with other human beings and participating in a common experience.

Once again, let's compare the movies. The screen is a medium designed for private fantasies, not for public communion. If someone sits down next to you in a movie theatre, you are inclined to move to another seat. You want to be alone with your fantasies, not share them, which is why you do not mind seeing movies in your living room or bedroom, and why film is the medium of choice for pornography. The theatre is more public. If a theatre seat next to you is empty, you think there is something wrong with the play. How often does one applaud or bravo a performance in a movie house as compared with a theatre performance? Why waste energy cheering images reproduced on a piece of celluloid? They have no idea that you are even there.

For no matter how brilliant the film, it was made in the past and it exists in only two dimensions. (I do not count three-dimensional IMAX, which requires plastic glasses to view a collection of scenic thrills provided largely by helicopters flown by stunt pilots.) In the movie house, no living humans come between you and your thoughts. No mistakes occur. Actors do not forget their entrances, or lose their props. The set does not wobble, the doors never jam. None of the untidiness and surprise and unpredictability of real life ever intrudes on the perfection of the artifice. The whole provisional life of the theatre that so fascinated Antonin Artaud ("The sky can still fall on our heads, and the theatre has been created to teach us that first of all") is lost in the manufactured cinematic product.

You may find that a great advantage, but it is no substitute for the active interchange between the living actor and the theatre-going public. I admit that today's theatre audiences, aside from applauding the entrance of the star and laughing at a few jokes, are usually extremely passive and decorous during performance. Are they asleep? Not to judge by what happens when the curtain falls on a Broadway show. All hell breaks loose with an eruption of bravos and standing ovations normally reserved for a bullfighter who has won both ears and the tail. These are largely obligatory, a ritual of Broadway theatre going. They are a vestige of a time when audience members interacted regularly with the stage, booing, catcalling, and cheering actors with whom they were familiar.

Today, that kind of familiarity, usually without the vocalizing, exists only between subscription audiences and company actors, another reason for praising the repertory ideal.

16

The Repertory Ideal

I have talked a lot about that ideal in these letters (at the ART I used to give a class called "The Repertory Ideal," which some students renamed "The Repetitive Ideal"). Let me try to explain why it is so important to me and, I hope, dear Actor, to you.

First of all, resident companies have been the main home for actors since the sixteenth century. In England, the first theatre, appropriately enough called The Theatre, was built in 1576 by James Burbage (father of the famous actor, Richard). Before this, strolling players performed in various inn yards. But by the 1590s, there were more than a dozen public and private companies in London, the most famous being Shakespeare's Lord Chamberlain's Men performing at the Globe (the company's home until it burned down in 1613 during a performance of one of Shakespeare's plays).

Henceforth, whether in England, France, Spain, Italy, or Russia, permanent acting companies would be the norm, and resident theatres would be plentiful.

Whether the Comedie Francaise or the Theatre des Funambles in Paris, whether the Drury Lane or Covent Garden in London (or, in modern times, the Old Vic Company, the Royal National Theatre and the Royal Shakespeare Company), whether the Italian Theatre Company in Rome or the Piccolo Teatro in Milan, whether the Moscow Art Theatre or the Meyerhold Theatre in Russia, specific company actors inspired their public with the kind of enthusiasm now reserved for the most popular movie stars. A good record of this kind of adulation, and of the life of the company actor, is Marcel Carné's magnificent 1945 film *Children of Paradise (Les Enfants du Paradis)*, which chronicles the world of nineteenth-century Parisian theatre as seen through the eyes of two contemporary performers—Baptiste, the mime, and Frederick Lemaitre, the actor—and through their interplay with other members of the company. (A more recent excellent film chronicle of theatre companies is John Madden's *Shakespeare in Love*, with its glimpses into Shakespeare's writing process, and his relationship with fellow actors Burbage, Kemp, and Condell.)

There are, of course, disadvantages to writing for company actors, though these are the limitations of any collaboration. One is that actors tend to take advantage of their friendship with the writer by fattening or embroidering their parts. Like most playwrights, Shakespeare was obviously unhappy at times with the way his plays were being performed. Hamlet's advice to the players suggests that his author did not much like flamboyant gestures ("Do not saw the air too much with your hand but use all gently . . . "); or mumbled and swallowed words ("But if you mouth it as some of our players do . . . "); or loud and boisterous behavior ("O, there be players that I have seen play, and heard others praise . . . [who] have so strutted and bellowed that I had thought some of nature's journeyman have made men and not made them well, they imitated humanity so abominably . . . "). And he clearly hated actors who overact, those hammy histrios who "tear a passion to tatters."

It is hard enough for a writer to hear his lines read badly or with emphases that were never intended. What about the actor who starts speaking lines that are not in the text? Clearly, that annoyed Shakespeare (or Hamlet) a lot, too, though the process is common enough today in the form of improvisations and interpolations, usually by comic actors ("And let your clowns speak no more than is set down for them," Hamlet admonishes the players, calling that a pitiful and foolish ambition). Shakespeare would not have been a big fan of such irrepressible cutups as Robin Williams who, when he played Estragon in Mike Nichols's production of *Waiting for Godot* at Lincoln Center, embroidered his lines with quotes from popular culture, nasalized the theme from *The Twilight Zone*, twanged "Amazing Grace" on an imaginary Jew's harp, and improvised macho John Wayne impersonations by turning a rusty automobile exhaust pipe into a machine gun.

Pirandello had the same problem with actors, and wrote a theatre trilogy (*Six Characters in Search of an Author*, *Tonight We Improvise*, and *Each in His Own Way*) exploring the uneasy tension that has always existed between the written and the spoken word. He was one of the few playwrights who recognized, with tolerance (though not without pain), that the play in your head can never be the one you see on the stage. There is a wonderful scene in *Six Characters in Search of an Author*, after the Father and the Stepdaughter have played out one of the two short scenes the author wrote for his characters before he abandoned them. When the company actors attempt to reenact that scene, the Father recoils in disgust and the Stepdaughter bursts out laughing. It is not that the actors are changing or exaggerating the lines; it is just that, as the Father says, "You're not us!"

These are some of the disadvantages of company acting. The advantages far outweigh them. Actors who have shared resident theatre work for a while have a tremendous head start over pickup casts. The most obvious one is their familiarity with each other's work. If you have not seen a theatre company perform over a period of time, you probably cannot appreciate this sort of thing as much as regular season subscribers.

The best analogy is with sports. A team that practices and plays together for a long time, even one at the bottom of the league, will most likely triumph over a newly formed All-Star team. That is perhaps why the United States basketball team did so badly at the Athens Olympics. The franchise team knows each other's plays; the pick-up team does not. (The ART once exploited this analogy by advertising its coming season with an endorsement from the Boston Celtics that featured a photograph of one of its stars asking, "Who makes the best plays in Boston?"). Many all-star productions—most notably the Actors Studio *Three Sisters* when it went to London with George C. Scott, Kim Stanley, and Geraldine Page—have sometimes been hooted off the stage, but company productions of the same play—such as the 1924 Moscow Art Theatre version or the 1957 Old Vic version—have left an indelible mark on theatre history.

The importance of these two elements, ensemble company acting and good classical training, was nowhere better demonstrated than in two failed American companies in the 1960s—the Lincoln Center Company under the direction of Elia Kazan and Robert Whitehead, and the Actors Studio Company under the direction of Lee Strasberg. When their Method-trained actors were performing in contemporary American plays such as those of Arthur Miller, S. N. Behrman, and Eugene O'Neill, the work was reasonably persuasive. The moment they stepped into unfamiliar territory, such as Kazan's production of Middleton's *Changeling* or Strasberg's production of Chekhov's *Three Sisters*, the results were catastrophic. The actors did not know how to develop the "masks used in the drama." Not only were they improperly trained in roles remote from themselves in time and temperament but they were not really prepared to work together as a cohesive ensemble rather than as a disjointed assembly of stars.

With the development of the National Endowment for the Arts and the beginning of limited federal subsidy in the mid-1960s, genuine repertory theatre models began to evolve, though New York was never able to sustain a company of its own for very long. Following the lead of the Federal Theatre in its effort to decentralize American theatre in the 1930s, most of these companies were established in cities throughout the nation.

Why couldn't New York create and sustain a first-rate theatre company? Well, for one thing, theatres are not day lilies. They do not spring into being overnight. Like English gardens, they need a lot of nourishing, watering, and weeding. New York is a flower market, not a garden. It buys finished products, not maturing buds and blossoms. When the first Lincoln Center Theatre company was created under the directorship of Elia Kazan and Robert Whitehead, with Arthur Miller as its resident playwright, some people (including me) began demanding instant results, and, when they failed to provide them, the directors were obliged to resign before the end of their second year.

Some people (again including me) believed that the Lincoln Center leadership was too imbued with commercial Broadway values ever to understand the requirements of a not-for-profit theatre. But most succeeding administrations at the Vivian Beaumont in Lincoln Center, even those with considerable repertory theatre experience such as Herbert Blau and Jules Irving (they had previously founded the estimable Actors Workshop in San Francisco), somehow never managed to establish a successful permanent company devoted to exciting new plays and unconventional reworkings of the classics.

The man who came closest to making Lincoln Center work was Joe Papp when he had the inspired idea of pairing familiar classics (designed to please large audiences) with daring directors (designed to please the cognoscenti). But after two years, Papp tired of uptown audiences and of a showcase theatre that was draining most of his New York Public Theater funds. Today, it is being run pretty much like the Roundabout, importing stars to do established classics and the occasional new play, then extending the run in a Broadway theatre if the production is popular.

Building a company is a deliberate process that requires time and toil, and, above all, deep commitment, rather like building a cathedral. As the poet Heinrich

Heine once said, "The reason we no longer build Gothic cathedrals is because they were built from convictions, and we have only opinions." That may be why no one has yet managed to start a lasting repertory company from scratch in the city of New York. Such efforts become the easy targets of opinion makers, not the calling of people with deep convictions. New York remains the only major metropolis in the Western world that does not have a major not-for-profit permanent acting company—though efforts continue to be made.

So, dear Actor, if you want to join a permanent company, be prepared to leave New York. If you stay in the city, you will have to take your chances with the numerous not-for-profit theatres that are likely to hire you there on a show-by-show basis: Among the best are the Public Theater, the Classic Stage Company, the MCC Theater, the Manhattan Theatre Club, Playwrights Horizons, the Signature Theatre, the Second Stage, and the New York Theatre Workshop. Do not expect to be well paid in these establishments, even if you are lucky enough to be offered a job. Equity minimums are considerably lower at off- and off-off-Broadway houses than at LORT theatres in cities such as Chicago or Houston. That may be because Equity recognizes that they offer you the opportunity of a "showcase" for critics and agents and casting directors who would otherwise not see your work.

I know of few people (Ruth Malaczech of Mabou Mines, having steadfastly refused to join Equity, is one exception) who actually choose to be freelance off-Broadway actors. It is just a way of staying in the "business" while you find ways to supplement your income through television spots, commercials (or industrials), or similar forms of employment.

So, let's say I have talked you into working with a company, and let's say you have been offered a season contract. Are you happy? You should be. For a year at least you are out of the New York rat race and enjoying the rarest thing in an actor's life: security.

After you have signed your contract and met your fellow actors, I suggest you take a moment and wander into the construction shops. Say hello to the people who will be creating the sets you act in, the props you use, the costumes and makeup you wear. They are the unsung heroes of the theatre. They are also important to your performance. A wigmaker or a costume builder can spell the difference between your looking like a derelict or a diva. Your fittings can be almost as crucial to your acting as your rehearsals. You should also meet, if you haven't already, the company manager and the casting director, who are often the same person. Quite often, that individual is the glue that holds the company together, the parent to whom actors go with all their troubles. And finally, go meet the person who employed you, the artistic director.

IV.

Working There

17

Actors and Management

I have mentioned a few advantages of company over pickup work. Here is another. In theory, the commercial theatre is run from the top down by a producer motivated by profits and interested only in hits. In theory, the not-for-profit theatre is run from the bottom up by a collective motivated by a love of the theatre and interested only in great works of art. In short, so the theory goes, one of these structures is influenced by capitalism, the other by socialism. One is oriented towards the audience, the other towards the actor. One is obsessed with inflating the bottom line, the other with cultivating talent.

Well, that's the theory. The reality may be different. There have been commercial producers—Robert Whitehead, Roger Stevens, Margo Lion, and Rocco Landesman are examples—who, although committed to bringing in profits, are just as interested in creating a good product, if not a work of art. And there are many not-for-profit artistic directors who have their eyes fixed on the main chance, which is to say a successful New

York transfer for their productions and eventually a commercial career for themselves. Some of the most successful directors on Broadway started as artistic directors of resident theatres. As Gerry Schoenfeld, the Shubert Organization's president, once said (comically paraphrasing Irving Berlin), "There's no profit like nonprofit."

Actually, the artistic director genuinely devoted to the best works of art performed by the finest resident company is a breed that is dying out. As I mentioned, financial pressures, increased by the loss of subsidies, have changed the nature of the resident theatre in many ways. It is sometimes difficult to see a difference between the profit theatre and the nonprofit theatre in their choice of plays, actors, and directors. When you look at a roster of the most successful, and sometimes most prestigious, plays on Broadway, the majority come from off-Broadway or the resident theatre. (The opposite is also sometimes true—the schedules of many resident theatres are now chockfull of Broadway and off-Broadway hits and revivals.)

It must also be admitted that if the resident theatre derives from a collective idea, it also owes something to an autocracy in being headed by a strong leader. With a few exceptions, such as the Living Theater, which pretended to be totally egalitarian when it was actually quite authoritarian (at least in relation to its audience), theatre is a hierarchy with one person at the top. One always hopes that, unlike most absolute rules, the theatrical autocracy is a benevolent one. Tales abound of artistic despots who made life hell for everyone around them. But regardless of style, the artistic director of a resident theatre is generally responsible for all creative decisions. He or she will choose the plays for a season, not to mention the people who will direct them. And although the director of each play is deeply involved in the choice of cast, designers, and interpretation, it is the artistic director who, at least in theory, will have the final say.

Many actors chafe against this hierarchical structure because it makes them feel overly subject to other people's decisions. Not having sufficient control over their own fates is one of the most frequent complaints one hears from actors about management. Too often, actors feel at the mercy of arbitrary and sometimes capricious decisions. Unless you are a star of the first magnitude, you are not in a position to choose your own roles or cast your own season. So it is not unusual to feel that those who make those choices, whether the artistic director, the play's director, or the casting director, are not sufficiently conscious of your capabilities, and not sufficiently courageous to take a gamble on you. This is one of the most delicate dynamics in the resident theatre, and each situation is bound to be different.

In the 1960s, undergraduates used to stage sit-ins "to have a say in the decisions that affect our lives." Actors do not have this option. The actor's relationship to authority has always evoked poignant echoes for me of Nora's relationship to her husband, Torvald, in *A Doll's House.* She also chafed under a dependent relationship with a powerful authority figure. Until she took responsibility for her own life, she could not be a fit wife and mother. Unfortunately, she had to leave home to make this happen. Must the actor leave the artistic home in search of full independence?

It would certainly be a happier situation all around if actors could make their own decisions about roles and plays rather than wait for dictates from Mt. Olympus.

Occasionally, there have been efforts to form an actors' theatre that would function as a true collective, all decisions being made by the company itself. This sounds great on paper. In practice, it is a recipe for potential disaster. Try to imagine a structure in which everyone is completely free to satisfy his or her will. You are actually imagining a state of nature, which in the political world is called anarchy. The ART once did a play called *They All Want to Play Hamlet.* That is an apt, if rather cruel, description of an actors' collective.

The most effective artistic director is he or she who can keep an eye on the needs of the entire acting community, making certain that each actor is being treated as a developing individual in need of continuing growth and fulfillment. (Even that sounds a little like a parental relationship.) This species of artistic director functions very much like an air traffic controller in a huge airport, or a train director in a railroad station, making sure the planes or trains arrive and depart on time, and trying to avoid collisions.

The person, in my experience, who did this best was William Ball, former director (and founder) of the American Conservatory Theatre. He maintained a loyal company of over forty actors, tracking their roles from play to play, from season to season, soothing hurt egos, and refreshing the company with new faces from time to time through his conservatory training. If people had grievances, the public did not know about them. And the way the ACT actors stayed with the company year after year testified to a truly caring administrative structure.

The trouble was that the ACT, under Ball, after an initial period when the company was truly breaking new ground, eventually grew extremely stodgy and conservative. In the 1960s, the ACT was known for remaking ancient and modern classics, including a dizzying *Tartuffe* in which the very floor seemed to be off balance, and a breakthrough version of Pirandello's *Six Characters* in which the curtain rose on an ACT production of *Hamlet*, interrupted by the appearance of Pirandello's apparitions (an idea I borrowed and modified in my own production of that play).

By the 1980s, the ACT had fallen into what I came to call "cuckoo clock acting," which is to say acting by the numbers with lots of fanning and bowing. This approach was, admittedly, immensely pleasing to the public. At curtain calls, the audience blew kisses to the actors, and the actors threw them back to the audience. Watching an ACT production was like being present at a love-in. Unfortunately, it was not penetrating theatre, primarily because decisions were being made less to develop great works of art than to create happy actors. When Andrei Serban arrived one day to lead the ACT through an unconventional treatment of *The Threepenny Opera*, the company grew so restive over this experimental director's unfamiliar methods that it tried to throw him out of the theatre.

Actually, they were unwittingly imitating the plot of a Pirandello play called *Tonight We Improvise*. The actors, asked to improvise some scenes before the audience, eventually revolt against an intrusive three-foot director with a monstrous head of hair known as Doctor Hinkfuss. Hinkfuss, who is modeled on the celebrated experimental auteur Max Reinhardt, meddles so intrusively with the actors' processes through his pretentious theories that they are unable to act the scene properly. Only when they eject him from the theatre can they enter the heart of the action.

So actor-dominated theatre has its upside and its downside, and as actors are the largest contingent of resident artists, as well as the most needy, the situation can grow unruly. William Ball is one of the few artistic directors who had the resources to lead an actor-dominated theatre. Some artistic directors, such as Lynne Meadows of the Manhattan Theatre Club and Tim Sanford of Playwrights Horizon, run institutions hospitable primarily to playwrights: The writer is supreme; he or she exercises veto power over who directs the play and who acts in it. Indeed, playwright-dominated theatres rarely have resident companies lest the options of the writers be limited.

At the ART, with a smaller company that varied between fourteen and twenty-one actors, we were generally identified both by critics and the public as a director's theatre, largely because of the number of American and European auteurs that came to work with us there. The description was not entirely accurate, because one of the reasons we invited these directors was to expose our actors to advanced techniques that would inform and enlarge their skills as individuals and as a group. For the purpose of staging new plays and the more realistic modern classics, we had resident directors on board, such as David Wheeler and Scott Zigler, who were much less radical in their theatre techniques and much more playwright- and actor-friendly. Our goal was to be an actors' theatre, a directors' theatre, and a playwrights' theatre, all at the same time. (It is true that Robert Woodruff, my successor at the American Repertory Theatre, has modified this approach and now keeps only four or five members of the original company on seasonal contract; the visiting directors choose the rest.)

So these are the three types of theatre you will encounter—actor-dominated, playwright-dominated, and director-dominated. There is also the star-dominated theatre, usually run by Broadway producers, and often featuring luminaries drawn from movies, television, rock, or hip hop. A quick way to determine what kind of theatre you're in is to look at the photographs in the lobby. These will tell you who is most highly valued at this particular institution: the playwright, the director, the acting company, or the star. Your life as a resident actor will be better defined once you determine whom the artistic director listens to most.

Usually, a resident theatre has two heads—the artistic director and the managing director. The one attends to creative business, the other to subscriptions, budgets, fundraising, and staffing. As an actor, you will be negotiating your contract with the managing director, though in the resident theatre there is not that much to negotiate. Beginning salaries are standard, usually Equity minimum, and the various benefits—health, housing, insurance—are determined by the union. It is in the managing director's office, near which the company manager usually sits, that you will bring your questions about apartments and dressing rooms, your requests for house seats or free tickets, your complaints about being mistreated by the box office staff. In the rare cases that the managing director has an aesthetic sensibility—Rob Orchard of the ART is a good example—you can discuss your personal and artistic issues as well. And if you're unlucky enough to be elected Equity representative—one member of the company has to serve in that office—

you will be speaking to management on behalf of all your fellow actors.

Your concerns about your roles, your difficulties with a director, and all other artistic matters should be run past the artistic director, for it is this person who is the creative conscience of the institution. Your casting for the season or for a particular play has already been settled in conference between the artistic director and the director of the production. If you are dissatisfied with any of those decisions, speak up. You may not be able to change anything, but you should not be afraid to express your feelings. Timing is important. I would not advise you, for example, to make a big flap the moment you arrive as a new actor on the scene. But after you have been around the theatre for a while, and know the personalities involved, there is no harm in speaking out.

I did this once as an arrogant young pup with Group 20 in Wellesley. I had been with the company for a few summers in Unionville, Connecticut, before it went Equity, and though I was not one of the founding members, I felt a proprietary interest in its decisionmaking, especially as it affected me. When the casting was announced for the first summer season in Wellesley, I went ballistic. A new director had been imported who was not familiar with my work, and I had been cast in what I considered to be inferior roles. In one instance, I had been assigned to play one of the servants in *The Rivals*, when the part I wanted was the larger role of Sir Anthony Absolute. I made loud noises, and pawed the ground, snorting. I made boisterous appeals to the director. I hounded the artistic director. Eventually, I got my way and played a character for which I was about forty years too young. (I had the chance to play Sir Anthony again in an understudy assignment at the

Yale Repertory Theatre, decades later, when my age had caught up with my ambitions.)

I do not advise using this gambit too often, though artistic directors are sometimes impressed by an actor who is really passionate about a particular role. Your passion may not guarantee that you will play the role well, but it suggests you will take it seriously. Actors are often the best experts on their own casting, though some (me included) have been known to have more nerve than modesty, more vanity than good sense.

One older actor of my acquaintance, who shall go nameless, was never willing to acknowledge that he had passed the time when he could play leading men (he was in his late seventies). He was not very happy about being cast in "mature" parts, though he was desperate to play the aging Lear, a part about which Olivier has written, "When you've the strength for it, you're too young; when you've the age, you're too old." In theory, at least, the actor was right. If being an actor means wearing a mask, then all roles are theoretically interchangeable. But the most sensible actor is the one who, without accepting typecasting, recognizes that age, physique, and circumstances can change the nature of the roles one plays.

Companies willing to guarantee the same roles to actors throughout their careers often deteriorate in quality. The most famous example is the Moscow Art Theatre, whose members traditionally have an unshakable hold on the parts they may have first played thirty years before. (This kind of "tenure," familiar in American universities, owes something to the civil servant mentality rampant in the Soviet Union after the Revolution.) I remember when the Moscow Art Theatre returned to our shores in 1964 with three productions, including Chekhov's *Three*

Sisters. Not only had the physical production remained unchanged over the previous thirty years but so had most of the cast. The actors playing the Prozorov sisters had outlived their roles by many years. The play should have been renamed *Three Grandmothers.* From a historic point of view, the production was fascinating. As an artistic achievement, it was like being trapped in the dusty corridors of the past.

While we are on the subject of aging actors in companies, let me insert a word here about "going up" or "drying" on stage. This represents every actor's nightmare (Christopher Durang has written a play about it, aptly called *The Actor's Nightmare*). But it must be admitted that the older you get, the more likely it is that you will forget your lines, however carefully you have committed them to memory. Of course, you will not have to worry about this for years. But every actor, regardless of age, recognizes and dreads that moment when the next cue fails to come to mind, or when he looks at the petrified face of another actor who has clearly forgotten his lines. Even as experienced an old war horse as Laurence Olivier was always in mortal terror over drying on stage (he also had an irrepressible tendency to giggle). The worst example of "going up" I know of was the opening night of *The Iceman Cometh* at the National Theatre when that splendid actor, Ian Holm, made his first entrance, playing Hickey, and could not remember a single word. Nor could he respond to prompting from the wings. He just froze. The curtain came down, and the show closed. Holm did not return to the stage for ten years, though after he did, he played a superb Lear.

Sometimes such accidents can leave an indelible mark on audiences. Once when Alvin Epstein was playing in a short play of mine about a man who had lost every one of his senses, including memory, his face went absolutely blank and he could not remember a line. Some audiences remember that as a rare, almost Pirandellian example of what has been called "the illusion of the first time," the actor's capacity to convince you that what you are witnessing is a unique and spontaneous experience, when performer and part have become inseparable. By the time of the second performance, when he knew his lines, the effect was not nearly as strong.

18

Actors and Audiences

Because the spectator, in resident theatre, is a familiar friend rather than a visiting tourist, a different relationship is bound to develop between the audience and the stage. Here I am not just talking about increased familiarity with company and staff. I am referring to the disintegration of the fourth wall. Modern audiences, accustomed to a tradition of realism that began with Ibsen, are accustomed to peering at actors who pretend not to recognize their presence, like voyeurs snooping through an invisible window. But before the nineteenth century, no such barrier existed. Shakespeare's actors talked directly to the audience from the stage. A well-known example is the Chorus in *Henry V*, who sets each scene, describes each action, and takes us on voyages from England to France. But Shakespeare also engaged his auditors directly through his epilogues and prologues, or whenever such characters as Hamlet or Iago engaged in soliloquies.

As a result, the Globe company had an intimate relationship with the groundlings, who regarded Will Kemp's Falstaff, for example, almost as if he were a family member. It is for that reason that, in the epilogue of *Henry IV, Part II*, Shakespeare offered to bring Falstaff back in *Henry V* ("If you be not too much cloyed with fat meat, our humble author will continue the story, with Sir John in it . . . "). He did not keep his word. Falstaff fails to appear in *Henry V* except in the Hostess's account of his offstage death. But it is interesting that the playwright felt obliged to make the promise.

Nonrealistic theatre has traditionally broken the convention of the fourth wall, and resident theatres often make a logical extension of this development by engaging their audiences in extra-theatrical conversations. These can take the form of newsletters, pre-show discussions conducted by the artistic director or the dramaturg, or more elaborate symposia that involve playwrights, directors, and actors discussing a production the audience has already seen. Questions from the floor give the artistic staff an opportunity to learn how that production has been received by the audience, where it presented problems, and even how it might still be improved. In this way, audiences become part of the process, rather than mute witnesses.

But the interplay between a theatre and its audiences is not necessarily limited to formal discussions. Once a community has been established, it is a natural next step for a resident theatre to try to make the spectator the equivalent of another actor. Indeed, in most productions, the audience is the final actor, not available during early rehearsals, to be sure, but gradually added during techs, dress rehearsals, previews, and regular performances. It is the audience who tells you who you are on stage and how you are doing. That is why actors, at the end of the evening, or even during intermission, will invariably characterize the people out front: "They're really hot tonight." "It's a slow house." "The audience seems very young." "It's the usual Saturday night crowd [i.e., overfed and sleepy]." It goes without saying that the quality and kind of the audience will deeply influence the quality and kind of your acting. It can exhilarate or depress you, inspire you to new heights of imagination, or dampen your energies. Every standup comic knows this, which is why he often includes commentary on how the audience is responding to his performance ("Are you an audience or an oil painting?"). And if the actor is an improvising artist—like those, say, who once formed Paul Sills's legendary Second City troupe—you will depend on the audience to furnish you with ideas and stimuli. As Viola Spolin, a great teacher of improvisation (also Paul Sills's mother), once wrote: "Without an audience, there is no theatre. . . . They are our guests, our evaluators, and the last spoke in the wheel which can then begin to roll."

Every actor testifies to the importance of the audience in forming, energizing, and freshening a performance. As Lynn Fontanne once said,

> *When I am on stage, I am the focus of thousands of eyes and it gives me strength. I feel that something, some energy, is flowing from the audience into me. I actually feel stronger because of these waves. Now when the play's done, the eyes taken away, I feel as if a circuit's been broken. The power is switched off. I feel all gone and empty inside of me—like a balloon that's been pricked and the air's let out.*

In other words, the actor lives or dies by the quality of the audience response, which is responsible for the actor's very sense of identity.

Instead of pretending that they are alone up there on stage in a world where no one is watching, actors will sometimes be encouraged to break through that invisible fourth wall separating the auditorium from the stage and treat the audience as members of the production.

This procedure was carried to its most extreme lengths during the heady days of the Living Theater in the late 1960s and early 1970s. In such free-for-alls as *Paradise Now,* the Living Theatre actors, stripped down to loincloths, invited the audience onto the stage to join them in "group gropes" after having descended into the house to complain about their inability to smoke marijuana or to travel without a passport. Some people, notably impressionable undergraduates, happily joined the actors on stage in their underwear. Others had no patience with this invasion of their private space or private parts. The critic Kenneth Tynan once threatened to apply a cigarette lighter to the soles of an actor's bare feet if he dared to clamber over his lap again.

Tynan's reaction was entirely understandable. But the shenanigans of the Living Theatre were only an extreme version of actor-audience interaction. They should not be allowed to invalidate the genuine advantages of engaging rather than ignoring spectators in the theatrical process. To provide you with somewhat less obnoxious examples, let me mention Ron Daniels's production of *Henry IV, Part 2*, where members of the audience were invited on stage to join Falstaff and Justice Shallow at table in the banquet scene. They not only filled out the cast, they got to eat a good meal. In my own production of Pirandello's *Tonight We Improvise*, the audience filed into the theatre to find their faces projected onto a huge screen by the film-maker Frederick Wiseman, who was pretending to be making a PBS documentary of the improvisatory process. At one point, the actors joined the audience in the auditorium to watch a video about Sicily collated and narrated by Wiseman. There was even a minor Living Theatre echo when these actors pushed some spectators out of their seats to get a better view of the screen. Knowing the actors, the displaced audience members responded with good humor.

Indeed, Pirandello, and to a lesser extent Brecht, are the playwrights who have most vigorously championed the disintegration of the fourth wall. Brecht wanted actors to speak directly to the audience to keep it politically aware, rather than narcotized, about the oppression of the working class. He also encouraged a style of acting that was more like reporting an emotion than identifying with it, so that the audience would remain alert and engaged rather than swamped with feeling, as in Wagnerian opera.

Pirandello, less political yet more right-wing, wanted to break down the barriers between reality and illusion altogether so that the audience would never be sure whether an actor was acting a role or speaking in his own voice. When I decided to play the part of the director Hinkfuss in *Tonight We Improvise*—a character who, for Pirandellian purposes, was now named Robert Brustein—the broth of confusion came to a boil. In a long introductory speech to the audience (all of it written by Pirandello, though adapted to sound like my own views), "Brustein" explained that the text was nowhere near as important as the direction and that, as Meyerhold once said, "words in the theatre are only a design on the canvas of motion."

This was Pirandello's way of satirizing the autocrats later known as auteur directors, those free-ranging interpreters who seemed to be usurping the supreme role of the writer. But the ART had been employing a lot of these auteurs in recent years; therefore, Hinkfuss's words, as far as some of the audience members and all the critics could tell, were coming from the arrogant mouth of the artistic director of the American Repertory Theatre. Me!

This Pirandellian dislocation of reality was exactly what we had in mind when the production was conceived. As in the ART production of *Six Characters*, the on-stage acting company not only used their real names—Jeremy, Karen, Tommy, Harry Murphy, Johnnie Bottoms—but even referred to events from their own lives while they were in the process of rehearsing a real play; thus, the acting company of *Tonight We Improvise* was also identical with the ART resident company, giving the audience a chance to recognize many of the actors' distinctive traits. At the end of the play, when the heroine Momina, represented by "Harriet" (Harriet Harris), has a heart attack in the middle of an aria and dies, the audience was left in considerable doubt about who was the actual victim, the character or the actress. While the actors were taking their bows, Harriet remained supine on the ground, and Wiseman coldly recorded the event with his video camera. Was she dead or alive, a real person or a dramatic character? The doubt was compounded when two EMT workers rushed on stage with a gurney and carried her off stage.

Moments later, when the spectators emptied out of the theatre, they encountered an ambulance parked on the street in front of the ART, its strobe lights flashing. We were tempted to leave a message at the reception desk for those concerned about Harriet's health saying that the actress was in the local hospital and doing well.

What is the point of playing such practical jokes on the audience? Because they help to show how, if actors have done their jobs properly, performances can follow you home and invade your dreams. At its best, the theatre is not just an amiable pastime, designed for escape from one's everyday existence, but something that can leave an indelible mark on your conscious and unconscious life. Achieving that kind of impact should be your highest goal as an actor. Once you succeed, you will learn there are few more satisfying experiences.

Movies such as *Being John Malkovich* and *Adaptation* have attempted such Pirandellian devices from time to time, usually through the device of using real people in fictional situations. But only on stage can the identification between actor and character be fully achieved. I remember once accompanying Stella Adler to a production of *The Sea Gull.* Although Stella had never acted in this play (what an ideal Arkadina she would have been!), she had been teaching it for years, and she knew every line by heart. Nevertheless, at the climactic moment when Dr. Dorn tells Trigorin to get Arkadina out of the house because "Constantine Treplev has just shot himself," Stella let out a scream of horrified surprise, "Oh, my God," as if she had never read or seen the play. That response was a great tribute to the entire cast. It was also a perfect recognition of "the illusion of the first time" in acting.

The secret of achieving that illusion is to keep your performance active. Never must you appear to be simply reading written lines. Even a piece of narration or a choral speech works best when you give the impression you are recalling the images you are describing—or, better still, seeing them pass before your eyes. That is the great virtue of the process known as improvisation. By paraphrasing the playwright's lines with your own words, or by building on those lines to improvise a new situation, you are creating something fresh and immediate out of what is already fixed and permanent. The famous "I could've been a contender" scene in *On the Waterfront*, in which Marlon Brando as the ex-prizefighter Terry Malloy chides his brother for ruining his boxing career, was almost wholly improvised by Brando and Rod Steiger. That is why it stands out so vividly from the rest of the movie. Similarly, HBO's *Curb Your Enthusiasm* is successful largely because so much of it is improvised by the actors on the basis of Larry David's ideas. Those are the techniques that create "the illusion of the first time."

As further illustration of that illusion, there is a legend about David Garrick who, when asked how he managed to achieve such a heightened realism on stage that the audience mourned the tragic end of Hamlet as if it were the death of the actor himself, responded in the following way: Rising to explain his technique, he began walking up and down the stage, pausing for a moment to pick up a pillow from a couch on the set; he then began to rock the pillow back and forth as though it were an infant, cooing to it, kissing it, stroking it, and then, abruptly, throwing the bundle to the floor. Garrick's auditors screamed as if he had killed a baby. The actor took a bow and said, "Ladies and gentlemen, that is my acting technique."

19

Actors and Directors

Garrick was one of the most distinguished in a long list of actor-managers who controlled their own performances, chose their own casts, and determined the itineraries of their tours. He lived during a time when the actor was king (or queen), and enjoyed the luxury of being, to quote Ophelia's description of Hamlet, "the glass of fashion and the mold of form." That time has long passed.

If the nineteenth century was the century of the actor, the twentieth was the century of the director, the twenty-first already promises to be the century of the auteur. For although good actors will always be the focus of audience attention, there is no question that to a large extent the director has now usurped the primacy, and some of the luster, of the performer (also, in some cases, the autonomy of the playwright). This has been true in film since the beginning, where, even though the star's name appears above the title, the director is king, and the screenwriter has as much influence as the best boy (inspiring the "Polish joke" about the actress who tried to break into pictures by sleeping with the screenwriter). It is an imbalance that is relatively new to the theatre, and it has divided opinion. Some regard directors as egotistical intruders; others see them as prime movers of the theatrical occasion.

Whatever your opinion of directors, however, you will have to work with them, so it might be useful to know the genus of the several fauna you are going to meet, and how they function in various kinds of theatres.

First, dear Actor, you must recognize the existence of at least three distinct species of directors, each of whom regards you as an entirely different type of prey. There is the interpretive director, whose primary obligation, at least in theory, is to understand the intention of the playwright and realize it through the medium of the actor's performance. Then there is the conceptual director, dedicated to reinterpreting and refreshing existing works, primarily the classics, and so making them more immediate to the present day. And third, there is the auteur director, who is generally concerned with inventing his or her own texts in a production almost totally controlled by one imagination.

The interpretive director—best represented, say, by Stanislavsky doing Chekhov, Kazan doing Miller and Williams, or George C. Wolfe doing Tony Kushner—is the one best prepared and most willing to fulfill a playwright's intention and to accept the author's dominion. This does not always guarantee an absence of discord. Chekhov's famous protests to Stanislavsky, who, he said, ruined his work by using sound effects and turning his characters into crybabies, suggest that he was not always happy with the director whose name is most closely associated with his plays. Nor was Tennessee Williams always delirious about Elia Kazan, especially after Kazan demanded that the playwright substitute a happier ending for *Cat on a Hot Tin Roof.*

On the other hand, strong-minded playwrights such as Samuel Beckett, Arthur Miller, Tony Kushner, and David Mamet watch over their plays like anxious mothers, and have even been known to take over the staging lest some insensitive director introduce unwanted "improvements." In at least two instances, when Arthur Miller threatened to sue the Wooster Group for its deconstruction of *The Crucible*, and when Edward Albee halted a production of *Who's Afraid of Virginia Woolf* because George and Martha were being played by two men, the tension between playwright and director ended in the threat of litigation and considerable unpleasantness. Even as permissive a playwright as Sam Shepard refused to allow a theatre to turn the two brothers of *True West* into two sisters.

There is no question that the premier production of a new work should always be staged by a director who recognizes the sovereignty of the playwright and acknowledges his or her authorial right to have the play produced as written. And there are a host of gifted interpretive directors in the American theatre these days—Doug Hughes, David Esbjornson, David Wheeler, Michael Mayer, Daniel Sullivan, Michael Wilson, and Arthur Penn are only a few—who have the modesty and the skill to perform this kind of task well. The unresolved question is whether a play should always be done in the same manner once it has been launched into the world and seen by large numbers of people.

Pirandello recognized that it is sometimes necessary to violate the letter of his text to preserve its spirit, which is why he counseled directors and actors to change whatever was necessary to keep his plays fresh. It is the nature of theatre to be in flux; indeed, whatever seems innovative to one age often appears conventional to the next, and this is the fate of the theatre. You cannot permanently "violate" a play by reinterpreting it, no matter how harebrained the conception. The play will always continue to exist, purely, as a published text. The idea of the "definitive" production is a myth. It is more productive to look at the theatre as a dialectical process in which each production is a reply to a previous production, a kind of theatrical essay similar to a debate among critical commentators, each revealing another aspect of the work.

Indeed, if every full stop and semicolon of the original work are protected every time it is performed, there is a real danger of bringing in a coffin rather than a living organism. How much directorial reinterpretation is too much? It is an important question because it suggests the source of the most serious of theatrical conflicts: a living playwright meeting a conceptual rather than an interpretive director.

Following Vakhtangov and Meyerhold in the former Soviet Union and Max Reinhardt in Germany, conceptual directors have usually limited their interpolations to classical authors, which is to say dead ones. When directors set *Much Ado About Nothing* in Spanish Texas or *Measure for Measure* in Freud's Vienna, Shakespeare is not around to threaten legal proceedings. Almost all conceptual directors, among them Ingmar Bergman, Peter Brook, Ivo van Hove, Francois Rochaix, Lucien Pintillie, Janos Szasz, Dominique Sarrand, Andrei Serban, and Andrei Belgrader, usually depart from the customary setting of the play. Not all these people use the same approach in updating texts. One group, led today by Peter Sellars in a tradition dating back to Tyrone Guthrie, creates what I call "simile" productions, in the sense that the director starts with an assumption that the original period of a play or an opera (say, the Rome of Handel's *Julius Caesar* or the Seville of Mozart's *Marriage of Figaro*) is "like" the setting of a later period (say, the Nile Hilton in Cairo or New York's Trump Tower.

Another group, led by Ingmar Bergman, Peter Brook, and Andrei Serban, creates what I call "metaphor" productions, in the sense that changing the play's historical period is less important than finding the right poetic image for it—as, for example, the Beckett-like void that surrounds Brooks's version of *King Lear*, or the way Ophelia, in Bergman's *Hamlet*, distributes huge rusty nails instead of rosemary and rue, and, after she dies, remains on stage as a mute accusing witness.

The simile approach is external and belongs to prose; the metaphor approach is internal and belongs to poetry. But whatever the choice, in an effort to make audiences look at familiar plays as if they had just been written, the conceptual director takes liberties that would never be countenanced if the playwright were still alive.

Sometimes they take these liberties when the playwright *is* still alive, and that can make the fur fly. To choose an example close to home, and one that involved a controversial casting issue, Samuel Beckett once tried to get an injunction against the ART to halt our production of *Endgame*. JoAnne Akalaitis's production contained elements that irked the playwright (though not having seen the show, he was obliged to rely on information from his representatives). First, this *Endgame* was set in an abandoned subway station, presumably after a nuclear war, and not, as Beckett specifies in his stage directions, in a bare room with a door and two small windows. Second, it contained a short overture by Philip Glass, played before the curtain rises, though Beckett does not stipulate music. And third, it involved two African-American actors, Ben Halley as Hamm and Rodney Hudson as Nagg, a casting choice that was especially objectionable to a playwright who was unfamiliar with American nontraditional casting practices.

When he failed to close us down altogether, Beckett demanded that we take his name off the program and posters. We argued that this was Beckett's play, not one word altered. After a lot of legal exchange, and a great deal of publicity (which inevitably increased box office sales), the show was allowed to go on, and under the playwright's name, with the proviso that the ART publish a note in the program that included Beckett's printed stage directions and a statement saying that anyone who respects his work should be disgusted by the production.

ART had no disagreement with the argument that a playwright's intentions should be respected, especially those of a playwright as great as Beckett. The conflict was over whether one was obliged to deliver a play as familiar as *Endgame* exactly the same way in every production. Most people focussed on the controversy were unable to appreciate the director's reason for changing the setting. It was an effort to emphasize what was already implicit in the play, that it took place after a nuclear holocaust (the subway locale was meant to serve as a fallout shelter). Perhaps Akalaitis's treatment made this issue too explicit, more simile than metaphor. But the real question was how much latitude does a creative director have in staging consequent productions by living playwrights? How much creative input is allowed the non-literary artist in the collaborative enterprise of theatre?

The question is related to the age-old conflict between what Jonathan Miller calls "autographic" and "allographic" art. Is the theatre the product of only one individual, like, say, a painting or a piece of sculpture? Or is it a compound of many hands, each contributing a part of the whole? Miller argues that all art is allographic in the sense that time itself acts as an interpreter and collaborator. If someone restored the Venus de Milo to its original condition, complete with arms, head, and color, we would consider that a violation of a familiar work of art.

Similarly, when purists demand that Shakespeare be produced in exactly the same way he was in his own lifetime, what are they saying? Shakespeare left no notes to directors about sets or costumes or lighting effects. Indeed, he wrote only a handful of stage directions. One of the few facts we know about the way his plays were originally produced is that Cleopatra wore a hoop skirt, which is hardly authentic costuming. Would that sort of thing satisfy the academic purists? Should playwrights be allowed to extend their control over production beyond the grave?

Beckett's answer was to put a clause in his will stipulating that anybody who deviated in future from the letter of his text and stage directions could be hauled into court, which was tantamount to embalming his work in formaldehyde. But it told the world that living playwrights are sometimes willing to go to extreme lengths to protect their writing. Carried to its logical conclusion for actors, this position has the potential of forbidding women to take men's parts (denying us Ruth Malaczech's King Lear at Mabou Mines and Pat Carroll's Falstaff at the Shakespeare Theatre) and forbidding men to take women's parts (denying us Harvey Fierstein's delicious Edna Turnblad in *Hairspray*). It also suggests that non-traditional casting, which the not-for-profit American theatre considered the keystone of its very identity, could not be guaranteed to nonwhite performers.

The condition in which the actor feels most squeezed, then, is when there is conflict between two major creative forces in the theatre, the playwright and the director. To whom do you owe your allegiance when each is sending you conflicting signals? Who has the final word? There is no easy answer to this question. Everything depends on the circumstances, and particularly on whether you are performing in the premiere of a new play or a revival.

The related issue of to whom the artistic director owes the most allegiance was forced at the ART once when I had a flap with Andrei Serban over his casting of *Twelfth Night*. His favorite actress, Cherry Jones, was playing Viola, and he had chosen the lovely Diane Lane to play Olivia, an actress who had worked with him many years before at La Mama when she was a mere child. We had also agreed on Jeremy Geidt as Sir Toby Belch, on Tommy Derrah as Feste, and on several other company members with whom he was both familiar and fond. The problem lay with the small part of Sebastian, Viola's twin brother.

Twelfth Night was scheduled to go into repertory with Shaw's *Major Barbara*, which was being staged by another director (Michael Engler) who wanted company member Stephen Skybell for the important role of Stephen Undershaft. I thought that Skybell would also make an excellent Sebastian (he and Cherry could have been twins) in *Twelfth Night*, and I was not eager, both for financial and company reasons, to commit a full salary to another actor, as Serban demanded, who would play one small part in a single production. I tried my best to persuade the stubborn Serban to accept Skybell, and when he refused, I ordered it. Serban, like Achilles, sulked in his tent for a few days without returning my calls. Three days before the first reading, he still had not signed his contract.

I felt the production was in jeopardy. If Serban walked out on us, the ART would be left with a leaderless show. As a result, and after Serban continued to refuse my calls, our casting director Jan Geidt and I delivered a note to his house saying that he was being removed as director of *Twelfth Night*. That caught his attention, and within the hour he was on the phone saying he had fully intended to sign his contract and that he would, albeit reluctantly, accept Skybell as Sebastian. He proceeded to deliver an extraordinary production, indeed one of his best, that was not only visually exquisite but that fully explored the ambiguous sexual relationship between Viola disguised as a male and the erotically aroused Lady Olivia. Skybell's performance was first rate, and Serban even gave him a mischievous scene in which Sebastian and Antonio, discussing their friendship in a gay bar, are overheard by an actor made up as Shakespeare, who writes down their dialogue, presumably for some future play.

We were all truly delighted with the production, but Serban was not at all delighted with me, despite our long association and my constant support of his work. He believed I had intruded in an authoritarian manner on his creative process. I mention this because sometimes the only ombudsman in a position to mediate between the actor and the director is the artistic director. In this dispute, I had been willing to risk losing a close friend and valued associate, and even endanger a production, rather than submit to what struck me as an arbitrary (and expensive) casting decision.

Do not assume that you will be guaranteed such protections when similar situations arise. You cannot always expect to be treated like a cherished family member, even in a resident company. Usually, if the artistic director has to make a choice between replacing an actor or upsetting the director, it is the actor who has to go. It is not hard to understand who is the more expendable. After all, a director is responsible for all aspects of production, the actor only for one role. If you feel vulnerable as an actor, that is because you are. An actor is not indispensable. There are always a hundred or more Equity members waiting around to take your job.

I am sure this makes the theatre sound like a state of nature, "red in tooth and claw," where leaders behave in a manner more appropriate to the corporate world than to an artistic institution. And sometimes, for all our efforts to create a humane atmosphere, the not-for-profit theatre does unwittingly reflect the conditions found in "the real world." On the other hand, you are much more likely to find a protective environment if you have spent some time with a company. We had an unspoken rule, both at the YRT and the ART, that no actors would be dismissed because a director was dissatisfied with his or her performance. If we had made a casting error, it was our obligation to improve that performance, not just to erase it. And the extra attention paid off most of the time, though not always.

On the few occasions we were actually forced to replace an actor, it was usually because of unprofessional behavior disruptive of the whole. For example, we once hired a distinguished Irish actor to play James Tyrone Sr. in O'Neill's *Long Day's Journey into Night*. Because of his movie career, this man had not been on stage for many years, often an ominous sign, though he was always strong and effective on screen. After a few weeks of rehearsal, it became clear that he was having considerable difficulty learning his lines. We were opening this production for a two-week run at the Hartman Theatre in Stamford before it came to Cambridge, and four days before opening, he still had not memorized any of the speeches in this long part.

Someone thought of feeding him his lines by way of a computerized teleprompter hidden on a table in the Tyrone living room. This allowed the actor to get through his part, but did not particularly encourage him to memorize it. Also, audiences were probably wondering what a computer was doing in a New London house in the early part of the nineteenth century. Anyway, the Hartman management rightly grew upset over the restiveness of the audience, and our own negligence, and we had to tell this distinguished old actor that he was being replaced in the part. The man was devastated.

The case of the Irish actor was an example of incompetence, which is why he was let go. More often, actors are fired as a result of too much temperament or bad chemistry with a director, and occasionally because of bad habits, such as habitual drinking or drug taking. An artistic director has to measure at what point an actor's behavior disturbs the artistic atmosphere more than it contributes to it, something that is true not just of actors but of all workers in the theatre. Usually, a long meeting in the artistic director's office, either with or without the director, can elicit the reasons for an actor's bad behavior. Talking candidly about the problem usually helps resolve it. I can remember only three or four instances in all my years in the theatre when we actually had to replace an actor at a director's insistence.

I have more vivid memories of a time when a director replaced us—by walking out on the company after two or three days of rehearsal. This was the world-famous Russian artist Yuri Lyubimov, whose celebrated production of Mikhail Bulgakov's *The Master and Margarita* we had proudly scheduled for our 1987 season. Before he came, Lyubimov had begun making the kind of demands that were no doubt easy to satisfy in a well-subsidized state theatre, but we were already straining our undermanned staff. Aside from insisting on a sumptuous apartment in a high-rent area of Cambridge and an expensive private school for his child, Lyubimov wanted a rehearsal space large enough to house a complete mock-up of his very elaborate set. The set included a pendulum that swung back and forth over the stage and the audience, so this meant a room of enormous proportions in height, width, and depth (not so easy to find in the local area).

Because he had been ill earlier that year, Lyubimov delivered his set specifications late, and he was late in auditioning our actors for his production (among the leads he chose were Tony Shalhoub and Alvin Epstein). But we were very happy to present him with a huge space we had located in the neighboring town of Somerville, where we had already constructed a mockup of the set to his specifications. On the first day of rehearsal, Lyubimov rejected the space. It was too dusty. He thought he detected the sounds of a subway running nearby. It was not worthy of a "master." Our technical staff immediately began scurrying around to find another space, and finally located one in the Harvard hockey rink. Acoustics would be difficult, but at least it was the right size.

Lyubimov reluctantly accepted this space, then turned around and told us that we would have to open the production two weeks later than scheduled. He did not want to rush rehearsals. A "master" should be given all the time he needs. We had another show in rehearsal, we had a subscription audience holding seats, and we had already sold a number of single tickets. I said no. Lyubimov packed his bags and left, telling the press that we were a bunch of amateurs unworthy of working with a "master." The entire theatre, glad to be rid of this demanding presence, breathed a huge sigh of relief. The staff presented me with a dartboard adorned with Lyubimov's picture.

As for the big hole in our season, our old friend Andrei Serban came to the rescue; in three weeks, and on a relatively bare stage, he restaged a powerful version of *The Good Woman of Seztuan* that was one of the highlights of the year.

20

Actors and Auteurs

This story suggests that directors have become so powerful in certain precincts of the modern theatre, and sometimes so impressed with their own importance, that they are often given carte blanche over the entire production. Total control is certainly the privilege of the third kind of director you may meet in your travels, the auteur, who deserves a letter all to himself. The term *auteur* has been expropriated for the theatre from a phrase the film critic Andrew Sarris borrowed from *Cahiers du Cinema*, suggesting that certain films are driven by one artist who puts a recognizable autographic stamp on them. The same is now true of certain stage directors.

It is significant that one of America's earliest conceptual directors on stage was also a man who later put his personal imprimatur on film, namely, Orson Welles. Welles was a child prodigy who began as an actor playing Marchbanks to Katherine Cornell's Candida (by coincidence, a decade later, so did Marlon Brando). He then went on to lead two companies with his partner,

John Houseman, Unit 891 of the Federal Theatre Project, and then, when the government shut down his production of *The Cradle Will Rock* because it smelled subversive, the breakaway group became known as the Mercury Theatre. Welles led a splendid company of actors, among them Everett Sloane, Agnes Moorhead, Norman Lloyd, and Joseph Cotten, who appeared in many of Welles's movies as well. But there was never any question about who was running the show. Welles not only played most of the leading roles but also directed and adapted most of the productions. As his biographer, Simon Callow, notes regarding his radio shows, his name was mentioned nine times in three minutes on the first "Mercury Theatre of the Air" without crediting any other actors, authors, or technicians.

As for his stage productions, he always imposed his own concepts on the classics by cutting the texts, transposing speeches, and rearranging scenes, and otherwise created havoc with the author's intentions. He may have been the first American to modernize a classic by updating the text and changing the geography, setting his "voodoo" *Macbeth* in Haiti and his antifascist *Julius Caesar* in Mussolini's Italy, always for the sake of "recapturing their original energies." Like later auteur and conceptual directors, Welles was accused by actors of being a militaristic choreographer, better at giving them marching orders than helping them find their own steps.

An artistic leader who dominates the headlines and announces to the press, "I am the Mercury Theatre," is not likely to hold a company long. On the other hand, many of these actors were happy to follow him to radio, and then to Hollywood, where Welles for a while maintained the semblance of an acting company.

Welles became a kind of hero not only to conceptual directors such as Peter Sellars and Andrei Serban, doing modern versions of the classics, but (after *Citizen Kane*) also a model for auteur directors, a burgeoning species in the theatre world today—Peter Brook (France), Simon McBurney (England), Ariane Mnouchkine (France), Robert Lepage (Canada), Giorgio Strehler (Italy), Tadio Suzuki (Japan), Kama Ginkas (Russia), and, in the United States, Richard Foreman, Ping Chong, Elizabeth LaCompte, Martha Clarke, Anne Bogart, Mary Zimmerman, and Julie Taymor. Many of these auteurs are largely preoccupied with staging new texts, often their own, or so transforming classical plays that they are virtually new texts. But a few of them, from time to time, are not averse to presenting a familiar classic in a relatively familiar manner. Elizabeth LaCompte does deconstructions of plays such as *Our Town* (called *Routes 1&9*) and *The Hairy Ape*. Foreman has staged *The Threepenny Opera* for Lincoln Center and Arthur Kopit's *The End of the World (with Symposium to Follow)* for the ART. Bogart has tried her hand at Marivaux and Calderon, aside from her own meditations on modern forms such as vaudeville, jazz, and, coincidentally, in a piece called *War of the Worlds* on Orson Welles. Julie Taymor works with Carlo Gozzi and William Shakespeare. This, however, is not the kind of work for which they are best known.

Perhaps the preeminent example of the auteur director—and of director-driven theatre as a whole—is Robert Wilson, a Texan who trained as an architect. Wilson is an international artist who has worked in every major Asian and European country; he is one of the most extraordinary figures of the postmodern period, equally adept at theatre, opera, dance, furniture making, and installations.

A totally Renaissance man of the stage, he has virtually revolutionized the way we look at the theatrical form. As the author of such works as *Ka Mountain and GARDenia Terrace*, *Death Destruction & Detroit*, *Deafman Glance*, and *A Letter for Queen Victoria*, not to mention numerous collaborations with the minimalist composer Philip Glass (notably *Einstein on the Beach*), Wilson has been a one-man theatre factory. He has not only been responsible for the text (with written contributions from the deaf mute African American child, Raymond Andrews, the autistic adolescent Christopher Knowles, and the German poet-playwright Heiner Mueller), but has often designed the sets, the lighting, the props, and the furniture pieces, many of which have been preserved at his museum in Watermill, Long Island.

Wilson has even performed in his own productions, most notably a *Hamlet* he produced as a monologue in 1995. But he can't do without professional actors, even though he choreographs each performance with the utmost precision. In fact, he often auditions actors by asking them to walk, sit, and turn according to metronomic time counts, which is the way he determines how well they can follow his instructions. Naturally, some actors have resented being treated as "puppets." Others have found his methods an open sesame into a whole new way of thinking about their craft.

Actually, once he has established his parameters, Wilson allows actors a great deal of latitude. Far from being a martinet, he is an extremely friendly and collaborative colleague. Wilson is always open to all manner of suggestion from whatever quarter. It is true that he does not have much interest in text, even his own, because he dislikes what he calls the "ping pong" of dramatic dialogue. But under the influence of Merce Cunningham, he has created a theatre of exquisite movement and striking visual tableaux that proceeds with the deliberate slowness of a dream to create a hypnotic and sometimes hallucinatory effect on the spectator. To see actors playing huge snow owls, grizzly bears, Abraham Lincoln on stilts, among a hundred other striking images, is to be transported into a world that is rich, still, phantasmagorical, and sacred.

I pride myself on being the first to persuade Wilson to take actors through a classical text, rather than a scenario of his own making. I wanted to see whether he could adapt his auteur techniques to those of a conceptual director. The occasion was a staging of Euripides' *Alcestis* at the ART in 1986. The ART had already produced the Cologne section of Wilson's monumentally successful, yet typographically bizarre, *the CIVIL warS: a tree is best measured when it is down* (Wilson's mammoth intercontinental epic). But this was something different, not only an established classic, but the first production in ten years that Wilson would originate in the United States. *Alcestis* proved to be a stunning realization of Euripides' tale of sacrifice, death, and resurrection; its exquisite climax featured Rodney Hudson as a winged figure of Death leading the transparent Plexiglas coffin of Alcmena down the river Styx, her mourning father (Jeremy Geidt) following close behind. In the distance, pieces of granite slowly tumbled down a far-off mountain, eventually revealing a future Golden City. When we toured this show to Paris during the Festival d'Automne, it won the prize for best foreign production of the year.

I next persuaded Wilson to stage a version of Ibsen's strange and symbolic final work, *When We Dead Awaken*, where he used such company actors as Alvin Epstein as Rubek, Stephanie Roth-Haeberle as Maya, and Mario Arrambide (later John Campion) as Ulfheim in front of an immense snowy mountain that became the site of a landslide at the climax. As an example of the way this director found and used actors, Wilson cast the great black dancer Charles "Honi" Coles in a small part after a chance encounter with him in a New York restaurant. At the curtain call, Coles, who had suffered a stroke some years before, led the entire cast in a slow dance chorus, all of them chanting the title of the play in unison as if it were a jazz riff.

After this, Wilson alternated original work—often musical collaborations with such popular culture icons as Tom Waite *(Black Rider)* and Lou Reed *(Time Rocker)*—with brilliant meditations on modern classics such as Strindberg's *A Dream Play*, Gertrude Stein's *Four Saints in Three Acts* and *Doctor Faustus Lights the Lights*, the Edgar Allan Poe–inspired *POEtry*, and *Alice (Alice in Wonderland)*, most of them in collaboration with the Thalia Theatre of Hamburg.

Many Wilson actors, paradoxically, feel liberated by the strict metric limitations he imposes on them. It is a curious fact that true freedom can be exercised only within a set of clear-cut boundaries. I have noted, for example, that set designers do their most imaginative work when they have a limited budget, or are forced to design more economically for rotating repertory, and that directors become most inventive when they have to invent simple solutions to problems that would otherwise be solved by throwing money at them.

So it is with actors. If you are left entirely to your own devices, it is possible that you will come up with a fine performance. But if your work is not being edited by someone with a clear conception of the whole, the chances are that it will not be coordinated very well with the performances of others on the stage. And that is really the first function of the director—to make certain that the entire cast is in the same play. It is the director who establishes the style of the evening, its tone and pace and rhythm. The actor who rejects or resists the director's instructions does so at the risk of upsetting a delicate balance.

This is not to say that you cannot have honest disagreements over the interpretation or direction of your role. And often it is the actor rather than the director who turns out to be right. Not too long ago, I invited a conceptual Russian director, Yuri Yuremin of the Pushkin Theatre, to stage a production of *Othello.* I had a lot of respect and affection for this great bear of a man who had previously done a number of strong Chekhov productions at our theatre, most of them with our students. But before long, the actors expressed their unhappiness about the way he was conducting rehearsals. For one thing, Yuri's English was not fluent, so his understanding of Shakespeare was limited (my fault for miscasting him as director of a play so dependent on language). For another, he had cut all of Iago's soliloquies (Yuremin didn't believe that characters should talk directly to audiences), and had decimated the fifth act, reducing the important part of Emilia down to virtually a few lines.

Miffed that their roles were being shortened, some of the actors had even stronger objections to the way Yuremin was approaching the play. And it is true that, in trying to find a fresh entrance into the text, he had come up with some pretty harebrained ideas.

His manner of establishing the atmosphere of Venice, for example, was to have Iago and Roderigo pull toy boats behind them as they engaged in conversation about Desdemona. The tension grew, and the rehearsal atmosphere became more and more unpleasant. Rather than try to ventriloquize my wishes through Yuri, I made the painful decision to bring in the more actor-friendly David Wheeler to handle the performance. Yuremin remained in charge of the mise-en-scene and the visual concept. I also asked the dramaturg to restore most of the cuts. The actors regained their equilibrium at the cost of the director's humiliation, which I sorely regretted, and the production ended as a respectable, though not brilliant, rendering of the play.

By this time, you must be asking why one would hire directors whose concepts are going to make actors unhappy. Well, sometimes the same director's concepts can make actors extremely happy. Yuremin once did a production of Chekhov's *Ivanov* at the ART, for example, that featured Arliss Howard in the title role, with his wife, Debra Winger, playing Ivanov's wife, Anna. Both testified that the production was one of the most fulfilling experiences of their lives. So did the audience. The pitched battles of the rehearsal room often issue in the shared triumphs of the opening night, where all tensions are forgotten, good will prevails, and director and cast embrace each other with undying love.

Still, there is no question that it is the interpretive director, much more often than the auteur or conceptual director, who gains the greatest respect and loyalty from the actors, and who appears to be the most concerned with their needs. I say "appears" because quite often this concern is illusory. Interpretive directors often have very subtle ways of achieving precisely the results they want from the actor. They differ from more controlling directors in the strategic way they make actors believe they reached these results by themselves.

The Brazilian-born, English-schooled Ron Daniels was a model of this species. "Yes . . . but" was his customary response to a particular actor's rehearsal contribution. The "yes" was the carrot reinforcing the actor's choice, the "but" was the stick suggesting how he wanted that choice modified or extended. This way the actor could feel encouraged about what was already achieved and inspired to take a further step.

With Elia Kazan, for example, the performance was never imposed on the actor from outside, or based on some preconceived directorial concept, but rather dredged from the insides of an actor's personal experience and psychic biography. This technique earned Kazan the reputation of being a ruthless exploiter of Freud's techniques—a stage psychoanalyst without a couch or a degree—but one who managed to evoke some truly powerful performances out of the very fabric of the actor's past.

Whether you find yourself working with an interpretive, a conceptual, or an auteur director, the dynamic that develops between the two of you will be the key to your performance. Unless you are the star of a one-person show, say *Elaine Stritch at Liberty*, and require only a traffic director to keep you moving on stage, you have no choice but to submit to the one person, aside from the playwright, who has the capacity to provide the production with unity. Everyone chafes over constraints on artistic autonomy, but compared with a dancer in a corps de ballet, whose every step and gesture are determined by the choreographer, you have a relative degree of freedom in the theatre. If you want more freedom, then become a director yourself, as actors such as Stanislavsky, Welles, Kazan, Mike Nichols, Joe Mantello, and many others have done. That is the only way for an actor to guarantee full control of performance.

Otherwise, dear Actor, be patient, strategic, and alert. Remember that, although you may not be entirely free to modify your performance once the show has opened and the director has gone home (the stage manager will be monitoring any serious deviations from rehearsal decisions), you can certainly begin to make it more of your own. And you, not the director, are the one on whom the eyes of the audience will be fixed once the play has opened, and they will stay fixed on you until the final curtain.

21

Actors and Playwrights

If you think relations between actors and directors are complicated, wait until you meet the playwright. Theoretically, this relationship should be harmonious, because historically the first playwright was an actor—a thespian named Thespis. Western drama began in Athens in the sixth century B.C., when Thespis first broke from the chorus and created that essential theatrical component called dialogue.

The dramatic material of this first thespian was based on Homeric myths. So were the plots of the three Greek tragedians who followed him—Aeschylus, Sophocles, and Euripides, all of them actors, too. The tragic myths had a religious base, and when audiences came to the theatre to see *The Oresteia* or *Oedipus Tyrannos,* they knew they were participating in a religious ceremony.

The origins of European theatre were likewise essentially religious. Medieval drama began in the church as a Latin dialogue called the *quem quaeritis* (whom seek you?) trope, where the three Marys come to view the body of Jesus and are informed by an angel that He had risen and been resurrected. Indeed, the very first director in European history was probably a fourteenth-century churchman, Bishop Ethelwold, who provided performance hints about how the trope was to be acted (example: "Let him begin in a dulcet voice of medium pitch to sing: *Quem quaeritis in sepulchro, O Christocalae?*"). Dulcet voice! Medium pitch! Try acting those typical directorial generalities!

Nevertheless, the Christian clergy, unlike the Greeks, soon found the drama to be vaguely impious and irreligious, despite its biblical subject matter, and kicked it out of the church. Theatre did not go far—actually right next door to the churchyard. Guilds set up stages in the church precincts and reenacted "mystery plays," which were Old and New Testament stories from the Creation to the Harrowing of Hell. And although the artisans of the guilds were often skilled in the particular mystery play they were staging (the shipwrights' guild, for example, which had the materials to build an ark, produced the story of Noah), they were not professional actors. Professionalism would come later. In England it would begin with the formation of theatre structures on the South Bank.

I mention this short history for two reasons: to remind us that actors have always been part of a mystery that has sacred religious roots, and to emphasize their historical affinity with playwrights. The opposite is true as well. Most playwrights have a strong connection to actors. Remember that, as writers, they have the option of creating more solitary, less communitarian forms of art, such as novels and poems. They have nevertheless elected to come out of their studies and deliver their work into the hands of you, the actor.

At the Globe, of course, Shakespeare managed to function both as a playwright and as a company actor (he probably played the Ghost in *Hamlet*), and his mastery of the two skills was no doubt partly responsible for his capacity to write such great roles. He mainly drew, of course, on his instinctive knowledge of human nature. But if his plays are loaded with rich detail, that is also because he tailored them to other actors in his company. It was not enough just to imagine the character of Sir John Falstaff. It also helped to know there was an actor in the company capable of embodying that monstrous tub of guts, namely, his close friend, Will Kemp.

Unlike Shakespeare, today's playwrights do not always see the advantage of giving their work to companies. Many of them would prefer to cast each role out of the roster of Equity members online in *Players Guide*. But that is a relatively recent development. For centuries, playwrights preferred to write with specific actors in mind, as, for example, Molière, a playwright-actor who wrote a series of wonderful comic parts, many of the best reserved for himself, and who died on stage playing one of his own characters (Argan in *Le Malade Imaginaire*).

There is no generalization that holds true about this relationship. But many of the best modern playwrights have generally preferred to entrust their work to actors they already know. It is true that Chekhov wrote plays before he met Stanislavsky—*The Sea Gull*, which put the Moscow Art Theatre on the map, had previously flopped under a commercial management. But all of Chekhov's succeeding works—*Uncle Vanya, Three Sisters, The Cherry Orchard*—suggest that they were written with Stanislavsky's actors in mind, including the woman (Olga Knipper) who would later become his wife. How else do we explain the remarkable similarity in age, type, and temperament between, say, his emotional older women, such as Madame Arkadina and Madame Ranevsky, between his sympathetic doctors, such as Dorn and Astrov, between his two unfaithful Mashas (in *The Sea Gull* and *Three Sisters*), between his innocent girls Nina and Irina, between his neurotic young men Treplev and Trofimov, between his oafish clowns Shamrayev and Telegin?

Bertolt Brecht also wrote his plays for specific actors, but not until he returned to Germany, after years in exile fleeing Hitler, to form the Berliner Ensemble. There he was able to work with actors he admired and a director he trusted, namely, himself. Indeed, it could be argued that Brecht was less a playwright than a conceptual director at heart, because most of his dramatic works are adaptations of existing works (*Threepenny Opera*, for example, is a Marxist version of *The Beggar's Opera*, John Gay's eighteenth-century play with songs). But however we label Brecht, with the great Ekkehard Schall playing such Brechtian figures as Arturo Ui and Coriolanus (in Brecht's adaptation of Shakespeare), with Therese Giehse and Angelika Hurwicz as Kattrin and Grusha, and with Brecht's wife, Helene Weigel, embodying Mother Courage in what is by common consent one of the greatest performances of the century, this brilliant German playwright had a company the equal of any in the world. Best of all, he had actors for whom he could write specific roles.

In the United States, the actor-playwright relationship has been more irregular. Like Shakespeare and Molière, Clifford Odets learned his playwriting craft by working as an actor. The plays he wrote for the Group

Theater—notably *Awake and Sing* and *Golden Boy*—were composed with specific actors in mind, people he had lived and trained with—Luther and Stella Adler, John Garfield, Lee J. Cobb, Morris Carnovsky, J. Edward Bromberg, Francis Farmer, Paula Strasberg, Art Smith, and Elia Kazan—who filled his roles as if they were tailor-made, which, indeed, they were.

Few other American playwrights have had this luxury. After the success of *Streetcar Named Desire*, Tennessee Williams kept writing parts for Marlon Brando into his plays—Chance Wayne in *Sweet Bird of Youth*, Val Xavier in *Orpheus Descending*, Brick Pollitt in *Cat on a Hot Tin Roof.* The trouble was that Brando decamped for Hollywood after *A Streetcar Named Desire*, and Williams had to be satisfied with substitute actors—admittedly pretty good ones, such as Paul Newman and Cliff Robertson. (Brando finally did play another Williams part in the movie version of *Orpheus Descending* opposite Anna Magnani, called *The Fugitive Kind*).

Arthur Miller seemed particularly partial to the actor Arthur Kennedy, whom he cast as Biff in *Death of a Salesman* and as John Proctor in the original version of *The Crucible*. But apart from that one actor, he rarely used the same people from play to play, and sometimes this was for political reasons; for example, he never used his original Willy Loman, Lee J. Cobb, again because he had informed on other actors to the House Un-American Activities Committee. Elia Kazan, the principal director of Miller and Williams, also named names to the committee. But he was much more faithful to actors, both on stage and on screen—among them Brando, Julie Harris, Eli Wallach, Karl Malden, and Maureen Stapleton. Years later, Miller would even let him direct his play about political betrayal, *After the Fall*, even though Kazan was the play's major culprit.

Sam Shepard is a playwright who, reversing the usual pattern, became an actor after having written plays. (He also spent some time as a musician with a rock group called the Holy Modal Rounders). But Shepard has recognized the advantage of using the same actors in his plays whenever possible. Ed Harris is a Shepard regular, as is the hoarse-voiced James Gammon and the muscular Will Patton. And he shared the writing, with his close friend the actor-director Joseph Chaikin, of various theatre pieces, in which Chaikin also sometimes performed.

Perhaps the playwright most loyal to actors in our country is David Mamet, who, by directing his own plays and movies, has virtually created a stage-screen repertory company out of friends and associates. Some of these were once his students—Mamet's legendary class at NYU not only produced a lot of young actors and directors, it generated a book about acting *(A Practical Handbook for the Actor)*, written by his students, with an introduction by their teacher. Some of the same students later started an excellent theatre troupe known as the Atlantic Theatre Company, which was dedicated to the production of new plays and Mamet revivals. (The ATC is a perfect example of how acting students who share the same values and the same training can later form a company.)

William H. Macy is a Mamet regular—he helped to cofound the Chicago St. Nicholas Theatre with him—and so are Macy's wife, Felicity Huffman, and Mamet's second wife, Rebecca Pidgeon, who has been the leading lady of virtually all his recent plays and movies. Mamet's first wife, Lindsay Crouse, whom he met at Yale while she was performing in one of his plays, was his first leading lady; she appeared in his adaptations of *Uncle Vanya* and *The Cherry Orchard* and in his movie *House of Games.* Other members of Mamet's theatrical family include Joe Mantegna, Mike Nussbaum, and his close friend, the magician Ricky Jay, who has played in almost every one of his films. It is remarkable that, even when he works on Broadway and in Hollywood, Mamet rarely uses stars, though he made one bad casting choice with Madonna in the Broadway production of *Speed-the-Plough.*

Mamet's loyalty also extends to a coterie of theatres where he does his premieres—first the St. Nicholas, then the Goodman Theatre, then the Vivian Beaumont at Lincoln Center, then the ART, and always the Atlantic Theatre Company—though he consistently brings in his own actors.

Because Mamet is an interpretive director when staging his own plays, the Mamet acting style is extremely minimalist. I use the word "style" literally because, although many of Mamet's plays and movies look realistic, they are actually extremely stylized. The clipped, emotionless approach he favors tends to make his actors look and sound the same from one work to another. Rebecca Pidgeon in *State and Main,* for example, is indistinguishable from Rebecca Pidgeon in *Heist,* though she is playing two completely different characters. William H. Macy maintains the same blank look of confusion on his face whether as a college professor in *Oleanna* or as a police officer in *Homicide.*

If you have seen Macy in other movies—*Fargo,* for example, or *The Cooler*—then you know that he is an actor capable of a great range of character and a variety of emotions. But Mamet, who does not believe in "technique" or "character" acting, works very hard, unfortunately sometimes very successfully, to erase all signs of histrionic distinctiveness from his theatre. His purpose is to create a world that can be immediately identifiable to an audience as a Mamet universe, regardless of the setting or the plot. His play about two upper-class lesbians in the early part of the twentieth century, *Boston Marriage*, is an interesting exception to this rule, as is his beautifully made movie version of Terence Rattigan's *The Winslow Boy*.

The Mamet style works quite well—as long as the acting requires little emotion. He prefers a flat, toneless delivery that seems to have been most influenced by Jack ("Just the facts, Ma'am") Webb in the old television series *Dragnet*. Macy's death scene in *Homicide*, for example, was almost comic because Mamet would not allow the actor to show any sign of pain or suffering, or any expression of emotion, even though he was riddled with bullets.

Mamet, who has always expressed distaste for auteur directors, has ironically turned into one himself. He controls production as tightly as does Robert Wilson or Peter Brook. The one area in which he differs from them—apart from his essentially realistic style—is in his relative indifference to visual design. Mamet prefers to have no scenic clutter in the way of the dramatic development. Considering his lack of interest in visual images, his work could just as well take place on a bare stage.

But let us salute David Mamet. He is one of the few contemporary American artists, either in playwrighting or directing, who have remained loyal to their actors and continued to employ them as a company, even when working in the ruthless commercial world of the movies.

That loyalty had paid off in a clearly recognizable and distinctive Mamet world.

And it has set an example for other playwrights to follow.

Stephen Adley Guirgis, a young writer about whom I suspect you will be hearing a lot more in the years to come, has been working with a group called the Labyrinth Theatre Company on such gritty urban pieces as *Jesus Rode the A Train* and *Our Lady of 121st Street.* A part-time actor himself, he collaborates with other like-minded artists, a splendid array of Latino, black, gay, and white actors, as well as with Phillip Seymour Hoffman, who directed *Our Lady*, in creating what is perhaps the first major multicultural acting ensemble in the United States. Playwrights working on their own cannot claim that advantage without access to an acting company where they can develop their work.

Of course, the most effective access and the best relationships between playwright and actor exist when they are one and the same. Which brings us to the subject of the one-person show. This mode of performance is a relatively new development in the theatre, though it was common enough in vaudeville, and vaudeville's offspring, standup comedy. Indeed, I have a suspicion that most American one-person shows can trace their roots to the confessional monologues of Lenny Bruce. In our time, no doubt because of the increasingly prohibitive costs of play production, the one-person show has become remarkably popular. It offers the advantage of a reasonable budget—one Equity contract—and generally no more in the way of physical production than a table, a microphone, a change of costume, and a glass of water. And think of the royalties a producer saves when the featured performer is his or her own writer and director. That is one sure way to reduce the number of spats between the stars and the production team.

In any given season, you can find between ten and twenty of these one-person shows on and off Broadway, some comic, such as Jackie Mason's *Politically Incorrect;* some sociological, such as Sarah Jones's *Bridge and Tunnel;* some feminist, such as Lisa Kron's *2.5 Minute Ride;* and some wildly improvisatory, such as Reno's *God.* Not all these shows, of course, are written by the actor. In *I Am My Own Wife*, for example, one man, Jefferson Mays, plays more than forty parts, but the person who conceived those characters was a playwright (Doug Wright). On the other hand, *I Am My Own Wife* is something of an aberration. More often, these pieces evolve out of the actor's personal experience and imagination, and rely on the actor's capacity to investigate the self in relation to others.

The late Spalding Grey was a master of this form in America, someone with apparently total recall about the details of his past life. It was always a pleasure to watch him shedding characters like skins while telling tales of his life in ancient bardic fashion.

This is not just an American phenomenon. Indeed, the Italian actor-playwright, Dario Fo, and his wife, Franca Rame, have both brought the one-person show to some kind of comic consummation. Fo's chief satiric target (in pieces such as *Mistero Buffo*) is the Catholic Church. Rame (in her show, *It's All Bed, Board, and Church*) takes aim against the subjugation of women. Both have learned how to use comedy as a politically subversive act, and Fo in particular shows you the glue that connects comedy through the ages, from its roots in medieval satire and the Goliards through commedia dell'arte and Molière to its modern culmination in such clowns as Charlie Chaplin, Buster Keaton, and the Marx Brothers. (Fo is indebted in equal degree to Karl and Groucho Marx.)

Let me cite two more examples of one-person showmanship, one American, the other South African. The South African soloist is the great transvestite satirist, Piet Dirk-Uys, who works in a tradition of theatrical transvestites that includes Dame Edna and Quentin Crisp. The offspring of an Afrikaner father and a German-Jewish mother, this fearless picador has been goading the apartheid bull for longer than thirty-five years, first as a journalist and then as a performer. For this purpose, he invented the character of the Afrikaner dowager, Evita Bezuidenhout, whom Uys impersonates in drag, his costume being a long dress with flounced sleeves, large earrings, sunglasses, and a huge headdress that would have seemed extravagant on Carmen Miranda. Beginning as a racist, Evita opportunistically evolves into the very embodiment of postapartheid South Africa, an inveterate reactionary who joined the African National Congress after the liberation. Lately, Uys has been using Evita to help educate South African children about the monstrous scourge of AIDS.

My American example is Anna Deavere Smith. In two consecutive shows, *Fires in the Mirror* and *Twilight: Los Angeles* (she has done others since then, but none as powerful), Smith has managed to bring her considerable mimetic skills first to an examination of the racial explosions in Crown Heights, fueled by the accidental death of Garry Cato and the retaliatory killing of Yankel Rosenbaum, and those in South Central Los Angeles, where riots erupted after the beating of Rodney King. In *Fires in the Mirror*, she accomplished the remarkable feat, through tape-recorded interviews with twenty-six diverse characters, of capturing not only the divergent views of blacks and Jews, but their personalities, dialects, and opinions in a manner that went beyond impersonation. In *Twilight: Los Angeles*, she moved among ghetto blacks, angry Latinos, Asian shopkeepers, and Beverly Hills whites, powerfully dramatizing a world of almost universal tension and hatred.

The identification of actor and writer in this form of theatre brings us back to the event with which this letter began—namely, the way the actor Thespis broke from the chorus not only to create the first dialogue in the theatre, but also to cement the union between actor and playwright. Rather than rivals or competitors on the theatrical scene, they are natural allies, and never more so than when they are one and the same.

22

Actors and Designers

We have spoken of the way the artistic director provides you with roles, the director with interpretations, the playwright with words and actions. Let's talk now, dear young Actor, about the way designers furnish you with your physical environment—the sets you inhabit, the clothes and makeup and wigs you wear, the props you use, your sound and music effects, the lighting that shapes your face.

You will meet some of these designers on the first day of rehearsal. During that initial gathering, you will generally be shown a model of the set and some drawings of the costumes. After that, you probably will not see these people again until technical rehearsals, when the sets are built, the costumes constructed, and the sound and lighting designers begin to contribute to the production. Do not be put off by how rarely your meet your design team, or how little commerce there is among you. They are absolutely essential to your performance.

It is their world that you inhabit once you get up on the stage. Until then, you are in a rehearsal room for weeks on end. You start with the first read-through and continue through the table talk, where directors and actors analyze the play; then come the first days of blocking, using mockup furniture and props when the play is put on its feet; and finally the run-throughs that precede the rigors of tech week. Now you are finally ready to leave the rehearsal hall and move into the theatre. This is a momentous time, rather like the first steps a child takes after months of crawling. Be prepared for really startling differences in the kind and quality of your performance.

I have seen productions that seemed destined for greatness collapse the moment they reached the stage, and never recover their footing. I have also seen shows apparently doomed to failure suddenly gain enormous power and beauty under the lights. Nobody can explain or predict this phenomenon, but there is little question that it has a lot to do with the physical production. The designers frequently function as virtual co-directors of a show. They contribute not only to its look but also to its internal cohesion, even its conceptual development.

By far, the largest number of imaginative designers have come out of Yale. Scene designers are developed in a program run by Ming Cho Lee, and assisted today by Michael Yeargan. It has produced such fine scenic artists as Derek Maclane, Riccardo Hernandez, and Douglas Stein. Lighting designers are trained at Yale by the great Jennifer Tipton, costume designers by the brilliant Jane Greenwood. Chances are that one or more of the design artists involved with your production will be Yale Drama School graduates. Yale remains the major training ground for artists of visual production.

Take Tony Straiges, who designed the legendary *Midsummer Night's Dream* I have told you so much about. Today, he is considered one of the visual poets of the stage. His *Midsummer* consisted of a huge wooden skateboard scoop in front of a mammoth moon literally made out of popcorn, down which the lovers and fairies scooted, slid, and slithered like children in a playground. I still have vivid memories of Christopher Lloyd as Oberon, hairless and muscular, creeping down this precarious wooden platform to gaze at the sleeping, half-naked Titania of Carmen De Lavallade, the shimmering music of Henry Purcell his accompaniment. Nothing in the rehearsal hall, no matter how intense, could match the magic created by that almost hallowed environment. The designers had endowed the actors with a sacred presence, an almost unearthly beauty.

Or take Michael Yeargan, our principal set designer at the Yale Repertory Theatre, and for almost ten years at the ART. Michael was my chief collaborator on any number of plays I directed, one who always helped to shape the imagination of the production. In my production of *The Sea Gull* at the YRT, for example, I thought that the entire action should take place not just near but actually on the beautiful lake that everyone admires so much. Michael realized this visually through a shimmering mylar floor that gave the effect of characters walking on water. For my production of Ibsen's *The Wild Duck*, he physicalized my concept that a subtext of the play was the replacement of painting by photography in the nineteenth century. He did this by dispensing with the usual stage curtain in favor of a huge camera lens that opened and closed between the scenes, accompanied by the blinding light of a flash bulb.

And I still remember one special moment, in my kitchen over an evening meal, when Michael Yeargan came up with the scenic idea for my ART production of *Six Characters* that totally fulfilled and refined my original concept. We were looking for a way to separate the world of the real actors rehearsing on stage from the eerie world of the six imaginary characters who visit them. Through pasty makeup and Jennifer Tipton's cold grey lighting tones it was possible to show the visual contrast between the real and the imagined. But how to bridge the two realities the characters themselves inhabited—their life in the theatre and their life in the author's imagination?

I knew I wanted a mirror on stage to illustrate Pirandello's metaphor of existence as a reflective surface that throws back at you unwanted images. Michael returned to his favorite material, mylar, a substance that had the capacity to reflect the characters sitting in front of it; and with the addition of back lighting, the mylar grew transparent, thus revealing another character—the pimp of the bordello—standing in a fully furnished room behind it. What is more, the mylar made it possible, under Tipton's magical lighting, for the characters in front of the mirror to be projected into the room behind it. Thus, they seemed to be sitting on a stage bench and on a living room couch at the same time, arguing with the pimp as if they were sharing the room with him, making the characters self-conscious narrators and suffering participants at the same time.

Another Yeargan touch was an elevated platform that we used for the death of the Little Girl. Pirandello provides the Son with a narrative speech about how the Little Girl drowned in a fountain. We changed that fateful location to a pond, and, to make the scene more active, had the accident happen before the eyes of the audience. A stagehand brought in a blue plastic sheet to represent the pond. The Little Girl lay down on it. And as the Son recalled in horror how the neglected child had met her fate, water began to seep onto the plastic as it descended on the elevator, completely immersing the Little Girl. She was then lifted, dripping, from the pond by the Stepdaughter, who, weeping, carried her off stage.

We needed a final effect in the play, one that would, in one synoptic image, sum up all of Pirandello's existential ideas. At the beginning, the six characters, back-lit in a blinding light, were seen undulating gently from side to side as a huge loading door was slowly raised. At the conclusion, after the Little Girl has drowned, and the Little Boy has shot himself, the six characters disappear from the stage, leaving the actors baffled and dismayed. As they wander out of the theatre, they make desultory plans for a late-night snack and tomorrow's rehearsal; "Jeremy" is left alone on stage to recover from his shock. "Kill the work lights," he says and starts to leave the stage. But everything goes out, leaving him in utter darkness. "Not all of them," shouts the irritated Jeremy. At this point, the loading door slowly begins to rise as it did at the beginning, and once again we see an eerie vision of the six characters speaking lines from the play. Suddenly, all six of them fall down flat on their faces. It is a gigantic two-dimensional photograph. "Jesus!" says Jeremy, and runs out of the theatre in a panic.

Michael helped me realize this final effect with the aid of a huge Polaroid camera at the Museum of Fine Arts, normally used for reproducing large paintings. We exploited the accuracy and precision of that camera to create an uncanny lifelike presence for the six characters, one that managed to persuade audiences that they were looking at three-dimensional people. That photograph became the logo of the production.

All directors love this kind of input from designers, and all directors look forward to tech week. That period is like reliving childhood and going back into a playroom filled with toys. Ron Daniels used to rub his hands together gleefully when tech week approached, eager to work with "me props, me lights, me sets." And there is no question that these toys absorb most of the director's attention at the expense of the actors. For the first few days, at least, when things are moving very slowly indeed from cue to cue, you are bound to feel neglected. All the work you did in the rehearsal hall to bring your performance to completion seems to be dripping away, like water down a sewer, as armies of designers and technicians take over the stage, sometimes treating you like one of those stiff little figures in their model sets. Who are these people? Isn't the theatre about acting? Why is the director suddenly so oblivious to your needs?

Relax. All the attention that has been diverted to the visual environment will soon return to you. After the lights and props and sound effects are in place, and the director is satisfied with his cues, you will have a chance to do some run-throughs and recover your performance. Not always, to be sure. Some directors become so busy with the technical requirements of the play that the actors may not have a chance to run through the play on stage until the first preview before an audience. Sometimes not even then.

Andrei Serban is one of these. He once did a memorable production of *Three Sisters* in which the first act setting was nothing but a bunch of chairs. That sounds simple enough for actors, doesn't it? Except that Serban could not decide how he wanted the chairs to be placed. Leaving the actors groaning with frustration, he moved them here, he moved them there, never satisfied with the arrangement. Finally, he had made up his mind about the chairs, right before the first preview. But that afternoon, at the final run-through, he turned to me, a mischievous glint in his eye, and said, "Bob, I'm going to play a little trick on the actors and change the arrangement of the chairs." When I started to remonstrate, he added, "Don't worry, I'll change them back. It's just a trick." Unaware they were being used as the butt of a Romanian practical joke, the actors did a lot more groaning. After the run-through, Serban said, "I thought this was a joke. But I like it, it's good. We'll keep it." The actors did their first preview on a set they had never used.

Serban plays a lot of tricks like this, partly to keep the production unpredictable. He has a horror of performances without spark and spontaneity. He is right. It is your obligation as an actor to keep your performance fresh regardless of how many times you have played the part ("the illusion of the first time"). And it is also your obligation to make the best of whatever resources you are allowed.

Even tech week can be of advantage to you in this way, if you use your time properly. When Rip Torn was playing in *The Father*, he spent a large part of the technical rehearsal apparently wasting time. He refused to perform unless an antique rifle on stage was replaced with a flintlock, and when this was done, he walked through his part making no attempt to act it. Instead, he used this precious rehearsal examining the props, refitting his costume, glaring at the other actors. At the first preview, we learned the reason for his odd behavior. Torn had been getting used to the room, turning his costume into clothes, making the props his own. This allowed him to give a performance of riveting power and realism.

The tech week is when you are first fully fitted with your costume, though you may have had some costume elements (generally in muslin mockups) for use in rehearsal. These costumes will invariably help you with your characterization. Indeed, they have the capacity to change your character radically. Ruffs, tights, codpieces, jerkins, gowns, and the like can give you a better sense of the style you are acting in than a thousand lectures on the period. And such imaginative costume designers as Catherine Zuber, Rita Ryack, Jane Greenwood, Gabriel Berry, Edit Szucs (a particularly gifted Hungarian designer who works with Janos Szasz) and others can usher you into new worlds.

The costume parade, as it is sometimes called, when you first have the opportunity to appear on stage in the clothes you will be wearing in performance, is the theatrical equivalent of a children's costume party, and often creates in the actor the same satisfying sense of showing off. We are all kids in dress-up once we get on stage; we enjoy the child's capacity to suspend disbelief.

I use the words *costume* and *clothes* interchangeably because I believe the best designers are those who recognize that costumes are simply the clothes of another period. Jonathan Miller's production of *The School for Scandal* at the Nottingham Playhouse made an enormous impression on me (we reproduced it with the ART company in 1983) because of the way it made its eighteenth-century setting vivid as an authentic historical moment rather than as an idealized re-creation. The aristocrats applied perfume because they smelled bad. The servants were pregnant and unwashed. When Lady Teazle removed her wig, she was totally bald, no doubt a result of venereal disease. Miller's capacity to imagine his way into his history, largely through the study of period paintings, and his use of designers gifted enough to recreate them, gave the audience a genuine sense of being present in another time.

It is true that many designers, obeying the demands of conceptual directors, do not always feel obliged to reproduce the period of a play. A large number of classical productions are now being updated to the present, or transferred to another period, or treated to a mixture of periods. I have mentioned "simile" directors such as Peter Sellars, who rarely, if ever, bother to locate a play or an opera in its own time. From a costume point of view, this can either seem a totally anachronistic indulgence or it can provide some thought-provoking historical parallels. In Ron Daniels's production of *Henry IV*, when Hal and Falstaff made their first appearance, they were sitting in front of a television set watching cartoons, eating stale pizza, and swilling Alka Seltzer. In *Henry V*, Daniels used a mixture of styles, the English forces dressed as grungy GIs, the French appareled as resplendent medieval knights and riding gorgeously decorated hobby horses. Sometimes this worked as a concept, sometimes it seemed superimposed. But Gabriel Berry's magnificent costumes, whatever the period, somehow always looked like real clothes, and they enhanced the actors' characters.

In addition to sets and costumes, there is the question of makeup, and (if you need them) wigs. I mention this because some actors cannot perform without these added hair pieces. When I asked the great Irene Worth to play a small part (Io) in Jonathan Miller's production of *Prometheus Bound* at Yale, I expected her to refuse. Instead, she accepted with alacrity, asking only, "Who does my wig?"

Makeup is also important to most actors, some of whom paint an inch thick, though lately I have found that many actors prefer to wear no greasepaint on their faces at all. In the days of footlights, makeup was essential: It prevented the performers' eyes from disappearing in the dazzling upward glare, and it also counteracted the tendency of some lighting designers to light the set rather than the actors. One of these, who always preferred a kind of Rembrandt chiaroscuro that made the actors disappear into shadows, was known as the Prince of Darkness. But the truly gifted lighting designers, notably Jennifer Tipton, James Ingalls, Michael Chybowksi, Steve Strawbridge, Pat Collins, Paul Gallo, and John Ambrosone, know well how to heighten the natural contours of the actor's features without the use of artificial colors. Make sure they do. Audiences often cannot make out what you are saying if they cannot see your mouth.

Character actors will always need their beards and sideburns and moustaches, in addition to their wigs, especially in period plays; and if they don't have time to grow them, they will invariably resort to false face hair. The first appearance on stage of a character actor in full makeup, complete with nose putty and false teeth, can be pretty shocking to the rest of the company. Faced with such total physical transformations, other performances have to be adjusted accordingly. For me the most extreme, and funniest, example of this transformation was in the movie of Neil Simon's *The Goodbye Girl* when Richard Dreyfuss was forced by a concept director to play Richard III as a flaming queen complete with a decided lisp, a swishing walk, and an enormous hump.

Another issue is padding. I am not just referring to such bosom aids as padded bras, the requirements of female actors stereotyped as well-stacked broads or buxom wenches. I am talking about fat suits. Certain roles, notably Sir John Falstaff and Toby Belch, require a lot of extra girth, and it is a blessing that light synthetic materials such as foam rubber have been invented to provide the actor with added avoirdupois without weighing him down.

If you will permit me another memory here, I was once given the assignment of understudying Falstaff, while playing the role of Pistol, in a repertory of the two parts of *Henry IV.* The oversized movie actor Thomas Gomez was our Falstaff, and he was doing a splendid job of it with no need of extra padding. But after playing the part for a week in Part I, Gomez decided that he could not memorize his lines in time to open in Part II, and refused to go on. That obligation fell to me, a skinny twenty-nine-year-old required to transform into an old tub of guts on only one day's notice.

I had already memorized the part. But as there was no time for the costume staff to build me another costume with lightweight padding, they quickly stuffed three or four heavy pillows inside Gomez's large tunic while the makeup man fattened my face with putty, freezing me into a permanent obese grin. We had time for only one rehearsal, an afternoon run-through. But being an outdoor theatre, we could only tech the show after eleven at night when it was still dark, following the performance of Part I. After the tech, which lasted until sunrise, I went to sleep and dreamed that this was going to be the hottest day of the year. And it was. The following night, I went on stage wearing my two pounds of makeup and twenty pounds of padding and sweated so hard that the dyed pillows totally discolored my skin. But I had the time of my life. Unfortunately for me, Gomez had his lines down by the next night, and I never played the role again.

As for props (or properties), these are essential aids to character, and you should request them as soon as possible in rehearsal. An actor without a prop is like a cripple without a crutch, and no amount of pantomime can substitute for having the actual article in your hand. In this regard, I cannot resist retelling an old story, no doubt apocryphal, about a performance in which an actor playing Hamlet came into the duel scene having forgotten his sword. For a moment, everybody on stage was paralyzed. How could Hamlet kill Laertes without a weapon? Finally, the actor playing Laertes whispered fiercely to the actor playing Hamlet, "Kick me. Kick me." Hamlet did as he was told and Laertes fell to the ground, whimpering "The boot was poisoned!"

23

Actors and Coaches

You are probably going to find yourself exposed to a variety of coaches and consultants during your performance career, whether in acting, voice, movement, dance, or stage combat. The coach-consultant can be an invaluable aid to you, someone on whom you can rely to plug the gaps in your training and help sophisticate your talent.

Unfortunately, he or she can also be a considerable obstacle to performance, and sometimes a serious pain in the neck to the director. It all depends on what kind of person has been chosen for the job and whether the coach is truly interested in improving your craft or merely performing ego exercises in the hope of creating a stronger position in the production hierarchy.

Let's start with the acting coach, a person who, in a sense, is a first cousin of the master teacher who dominates so many acting studios and drama schools. Dedicated to performance issues first and foremost, this consultant offers the same potential as the master teacher for creating conflicts with the director. Theoretically, of course, the best person to iron out your acting problems is your director, who has the clearest idea of what kind of performance he or she wants from you. But directors are usually concerned with so many other things that they may not always be there to give you the attention you need.

This is where the acting coach comes in. If the consultant is someone who has worked with the company, or the director, for a long time, he or she could be an invaluable aid. The job of the consultant, under such circumstances, is to translate a particular piece of direction into acting terms. Let's say you have been asked to cross the stage because the director wants to solve a traffic problem. The acting coach can suggest motivation for this move—say, that you would prefer to avoid another character who has just entered, or that you are looking for a more comfortable place to sit down.

This kind of advice can be of use in helping you graph the arc of your character development. The acting coach can also be an ombudsman between you and the director during some of the disagreements that arise during rehearsal. Your problems with playwrights are usually a lot easier. Most of them are perfectly satisfied as long as you say their words audibly, speak no more than is set down for you, and refrain from sawing the air too much with your hands. These things the coach can easily help you achieve. Most directors, on the other hand, have a clear idea of the kind of performance they want from you but may not know how to get it. The coach can help you there, too.

Sometimes, you may be given instructions that no consultant can help you with. In Molière's *Sganarelle*, for example, Serban once told an actor (Mark Linn-Baker) who had just finished a scene: "And now I want you to disappear." Mark started to walk off the stage, and Serban said, "No, I don't want you to leave, I want you to disappear!" Mark scratched his head, thought a lot about it, closed his eyes, and puffed out his cheeks. Still he remained visible, to Serban's chagrin. Finally, the problem was solved not by a coach but by a stagehand who rigged a trapdoor under Mark's feet, which, being sprung at the proper moment, allowed the actor to "disappear."

The coach can provide the acting equivalents of such solutions. Directions such as "Play it older. Play it angry. Play it like you resent being there" are about as useful to an actor as Bishop Ethelwold's "dulcet voice" and "medium pitch." They have to be translated into acting terms, into intentions and objectives, into questions such as "Where am I going?" and "What do I want?" Answering these questions is the specialty of the acting coach. Ask them too often of a director and you may find yourself treated like the actor who complained that a stage right cross he was asked to make did not feel justified. "What is my motivation? I can't make the cross without my motivation," said the actor. "Your motivation" retorted the director, with more than a little heat, "is to earn your paycheck at the end of the week."

The best acting consultant we ever had at the ART was David Wheeler. As founder of the now defunct Theatre Company of Boston, the breeding grounds of numerous later stars—Jon Voight, Robert De Niro, and, especially, Al Pacino, who always wants David around his stage productions whether as a director or a coach—Wheeler learned how to gain the trust and love of his actors. And as someone accomplished at staging plays himself, he always had the respect of other directors.

They knew that, as an acting coach, David was not in competition with them, but rather trying to help fulfill a directorial intention. David's solutions were always a mystery to me, but they usually seemed to work. Once he was staging a scene in a Harold Pinter play that did not have the required force or menace. "I know what's wrong," said David, and told the actors sitting in two facing armchairs to reverse their positions on stage. Sounds silly? Yes, but it worked. The scene played fine. Don't ask me why.

David's success as an acting consultant derives from his capacity to sublimate his own ego to the needs of the play. Compare an entirely different kind of acting coach, Lee Strasberg's wife, Paula, who, though nominally Marilyn Monroe's acting coach, actually became her manager, psychoanalyst, confidante, religious counselor, masseuse, and chief conspirator. Paula's presence on the location of a Monroe movie was immediate cause for alarm among producers and directors. When Monroe was shooting *The Prince and the Showgirl* with Laurence Olivier as her director and co-star, for example, Paula Strasberg caused so much conflict over the issues of Marilyn's performance that Olivier, upset by his co-star's "spikiness and spite," tried to have Paula removed from the set. The only trouble was that Monroe would have gone with her.

Similarly, when Monroe was on location with Arthur Miller's *The Misfits*, Paula Strasberg was almost responsible for the cancellation of the movie. Possibly because Monroe and Miller's marriage was breaking up at the time, Paula became the conduit for all of Marilyn's demands, usually cuts and rewrites designed to adapt the role more to Marilyn's self-image. Sometimes, Monroe would refuse to do a scene until after she had made a long distance call to her guru at the Actors Studio, Lee Strasberg. This drove the movie's director, John Huston, to the limits of his patience. And when Monroe, partly on the advice of Paula, began showing up later and later for her scenes, keeping the other actors waiting in the broiling Arizona sun while she was achieving the right acting karma, the tension in the air became palpable. Monroe's aging co-star, Clark Gable, died of a heart attack not long after the film was completed; some have suggested that Gable's poor health deteriorated even more as a result of Monroe's behavior. (Arthur Miller recently wrote a play about this relationship called *Finishing the Picture.* I wrote one earlier on the same subject called *Nobody Dies on Friday.*)

If this sounds a little like the relationship between George du Maurier's Svengali and Trilby, that is pretty much what it is. The actor, who can theoretically benefit from every type of influence, is natural prey for the wily scam artist or fanatical guru. It is up to you to exercise vigilance regarding people who would exploit your career, especially if you achieve a degree of fame.

You should also beware of the acting coach (or director) who wants to meddle in your psychic life. Sometimes, this kind of psychoanalytical investigation can have a potent effect on performance, as, for example, the playing of the legendary Kim Stanley (watch her playing Marilyn Monroe in extremis in Paddy Chayefsky's film *The Goddess*). Sometimes, such methods can create a bit of an embarrassment, as, for example, in the stage and screen performances of Sandy Dennis, who often seemed to be having a nervous breakdown right before your eyes. But even when this method is successful, it has the potential for dangerous results. Kim Stanley, who was positioned to become one of the great actors of the American stage, developed such a severe case of stage fright in her middle years, a result of the constant Method invasions into her personal life, that she fled the theatre and spent the rest of her career as a teacher in Albuquerque.

There is no question that "personalization," as this technique is called, can bring more depth and additional levels of truth to your playing of a role. But watch out for the coach or teacher or director who offers to play amateur psychoanalyst with you. If you choose to make such a journey, do it with a professional. The unskilled therapist can do you a lot of harm.

So the acting consultant is a moveable feast and a variable advantage. A voice or singing coach, on the other hand, can sometimes be a real help to your acting, especially if you are cast in a classical play or a musical. Tyrone Guthrie used to grumble that the only thing voice people were good for was to teach phonetics and help actors scan eight lines of verse. From his narrow perspective, their terminology and techniques were a mystery that contributed more to the art of obfuscation than to clarity.

I suppose some voice coaches—like some acting consultants—have abused their authority from time to time for the sake of their own needs. Most of the people I know in that area, however, have been invaluable and selfless colleagues. Elizabeth Smith, who started the program at Yale and then went on to lead the voice department at Juilliard, was almost legendary in the way she helped an actor shape and refine his or her vocal resources. Many of America's finest actors (Kevin Kline,

Val Kilmer, Elizabeth Mastrantonio, Bill Camp, Elizabeth Marvel) owe their commanding voices to her. Other fine voice teachers are Bonnie Raphael, former voice consultant at the ART and now at the School of the Arts in the University of North Carolina, and Nancy Houfek, who now supervises voice at the ART and the Institute. The contribution of each of these fine teachers to the voice production of our company and to student actors has been incalculable.

Where voice coaches can help you, aside from teaching phonetics and scansion, are in the areas of breathing, singing, dialects, characterization, and vocal physiotherapy. If you have a problem with your larynx—hoarseness or polyps or a simple sore throat—these are the experts who can recommend the right ointments and lozenges and sprays. If you cannot get through a long speech without coughing or wheezing, it is they who will show you how better to use your lungs and voice box. If you suffer from a lisp, or a stammer, or a glottal stop, they can provide the remedial advice to help cure your handicaps. If you need to play a dialect part—say the Irishwoman Pegeen Mike in *Playboy of the Western World* or the Welshman Fluellen in *Henry V*—the voice coaches will drill you in the proper accents or guide you to the proper dialect recordings.

Indeed, one of the dialects you will have to learn is your own tongue. Fashions vary about whether regional accents are a colorful addition to acting or a handicap. In England, for example, the Oxbridge, or BBC, school of acting, with its broad *a*'s and trilled *r*'s, pear-like tones and plummy diction, had dominated the first part of the twentieth century, largely through the hegemony of the theatrical knights, Sir Laurence Olivier, Sir John Gielgud, Sir Ralph Richardson, Sir Alec Guinness, and Sir Michael Redgrave, not to mention the theatrical dames, Dame Edith Evans and Dame Diana Rigg.

But towards the close of the 1950s, there was a major revolution in speech styles after plays written by working-class "angry young men," the most famous being John Osborne's *Look Back in Anger*, as produced by the English Stage Company at the Royal Court Theatre. A Midlands accent or a touch of Cockney in English speech soon came to be considered the sign of a more authentic and electric style of acting. When Laurence Olivier founded the National Theatre at the Old Vic in 1963, he was careful to include some of these working-class regionals in his company—not only Albert Finney, Alan Bates, Robert Stephens, and Colin Blakely but also the woman who was later to become his wife, Joan (later Dame Joan) Plowright. Olivier ends his *Confessions of an Actor* with a very moving and inspiring letter to Plowright in which he calls her "the rebel of the Royal Court, hobnobbing with all these stiff and starchy folk."

The same kind of transformation can be found in German theatre around the time of Brecht, who preferred regional dialects to the high German *(Hoch Deutsch)* then in vogue. And it eventually reached our country as well in the 1960s and 1970s. In the years immediately following World War II, many American actors interested in the classics had been training at British acting schools—the Royal Academy of Dramatic Art, the London Academy of Music and Dramatic Art, and the Old Vic acting school—returning to the United States with the accents of the English playing fields.

American acting schools created similar national confusions. When I was a drama student at Yale in 1948, we were instructed in something called "a mid-Atlantic accent" when performing the classics—not quite British, but not quite American either. I argued that the mid-Atlantic was a body of water where nobody lived, indeed where you were very likely to drown, so what was the use of speaking in an unknown tongue with water in your mouth? The voice department considered me an insolent pup which, of course, I was. But a few decades later, American actors grew tired of imitating Olivier and Gielgud and Richardson when playing Shakespeare and started to use their own native dialects.

The leader of this insurgency was Joe Papp, especially in his work at Shakespeare in the Park. I still remember my pleased astonishment after watching a production of his Central Park production of *The Taming of the Shrew:* Not only were the farce scenes influenced by American vaudeville and burlesque traditions but the language of the actors was something I could actually recognize from my own experience—homespun American speech. Soon after, many other classical companies began to Americanize their productions. And the vocal coach who had once been commissioned to teach you how to pass as an Englishman was now being hired for that purpose only when the company was performing Coward or Pinter or Stoppard, and sometimes not even then.

Aside from teaching accents and dialects, the vocal coach can also help you transform your voice to fit the requirements of your role. The most celebrated example of this kind of change was that of Laurence Olivier in his performance as Othello. He knew the Moor had to be played barefoot, and he knew his accent would have to be that of a foreigner. But perhaps thinking of Paul

Robeson, the African American basso who gave what some still believe was the definitive performance of the part, Olivier also had the conviction that Othello's voice had to be deep—"Bass, a bass part, a sound that should be dark violet—velvet stuff." Normally a high-pitched crackle, Olivier's voice production underwent a total change when he came to play the Moor. With the help of vocal coaches and his own determination, he dropped it an octave.

As for singing coaches, they are very useful, too, if a play has songs, to instruct you in the proper pitch and volume, intonation and phrasing. And if you cannot sing, they can teach you how to talk your way through a number, as Rex Harrison did so memorably in the musical *My Fair Lady*. In fact, whenever I think of voice coaches, I think of Henry Higgins in George Bernard Shaw's *Pygmalion* (the play on which *My Fair Lady* was based), an expert in linguistics who could turn a scullery maid into a lady through the proper application of phonetics.

Also potentially important to your performance are the physical coaches, namely the choreographer and movement coach and fight consultant. Now that musicals are considered "the native American art form," it has become essential for actors to dance and sing as well as to walk and talk. And if you are going to act in a play that features duels or battle scenes, you had better learn some swordsmanship, how to use a foil, an épée, a saber, and a broadsword. Being untrained in this area can be a danger to your health, especially as you are unprotected on stage by fencing masks and tunics. A famous Thurber cartoon shows a fencer slicing off the head of his opponent as he triumphantly shouts, "Touché." Without proper training, you might not lose your head, but watch out for your eyes, your nose, and your throat. B. H. Barry is the acknowledged master in providing you with safeguards, probably because he is a fine actor himself as well as a swordsman.

Speaking of movement, it is an actor's obligation to know how to walk more gracefully than other people and even, if the part requires it, less gracefully, the way Olivier as Richard III suppressed his natural grace and dragged his leg along the ground. It did not hurt Christopher Walken a bit that he began his stage career as a gypsy dancer on the musical comedy circuit before becoming a self-taught classical actor. (He read Shakespeare aloud to himself every morning.) Learning to dance well inevitably improves the way you move and walk.

Today, largely because of the popularity of musicals, many choreographers function as directors, staging shows where movement dominates production. Bob Fosse, one of the first director-choreographers, brought his rakish style both to movies, such as *All That Jazz*, and to shows, such as *42nd Street* (eerily, having predicted his own death in the movie, he died on the opening night of the show). Susan Stroman is one of Fosse's natural descendants—not just in her choreographed dance pieces, such as *Contact*, but also in full-scale musicals—*The Producers*, *Oklahoma*, and *The Frogs*. And Martha Clarke, who began as a dancer-choreographer with the company called Pilobolus, went on to create stunning theatre pieces, beginning with her mesmerizing *Garden of Earthly Delights*, a theatricalization of Hieronymous Bosch's paintings, that virtually started a whole new movement genre.

Clarke was also responsible, in collaboration with the playwright Charles Mee Jr., for a powerful piece about sex at the end of the nineteenth century called *Vienna: Lusthaus*, inspired by the sensual paintings of Egon Schiele and Gustav Klimt. With the same playwright, she created an evening based on Franz Kafka's *The Hunger Artist.* And she recently completed a production for the American Repertory Theatre of *A Midsummer Night's Dream* (a successor to the Alvin Epstein version) in which the fairies not only danced and spoke but even flew through the air wearing harnesses designed by the flying wizard Peter Foy. As you can see, actors these days are required to do a lot more than act. In our own production of Aristophanes' *The Frogs*, produced in the Yale swimming pool in 1975 with music by Stephen Sondheim, they were even required to swim.

Naturally, performers who are trained to perform, sing, and dance, if not to fly and to swim, are going to be those most valuable to a company that occasionally does musical work. The more versatile your talents, the more likely your ability to find employment. But few actors are triple-threat talents, and directors should beware of making excessive demands on them, or of overloading them with consultants.

This brings us to another question regarding actors: Now that legitimate theatre is evolving into musical theatre and musical theatre into opera, who are the most appropriate artists for the transition? The same actor who could handle a singing part in Stephen Sondheim's *A Funny Thing Happened on the Way to Forum*, for example, might be inadequate to the more operatic demands of Sondheim's *Passion*. Should coaches be entrusted to teach the company actors new vocal techniques, or should professional singers be hired in their place? There is no doubt that some musical works require skills beyond the talents of a regular acting company.

Philip Glass, for example, usually writes for opera singers rather than singing actors, even though his works are highly theatrical (he began his career with Mabou Mines). When we performed his exquisite *Juniper Tree* (written with Robert Moran), and his opera adaptation of Jean Cocteau's movie *Orphée*, we had to bring in trained professionals to sing the principal roles. On the other hand, the composer William Bolcom, who also has had a lot of theatre experience, generally likes to write for cabaret artists (including his wife, Joan Morris) as much as for opera singers. He once composed a piece called *Dynamite Tonite* with the playwright Arnold Weinstein that was identified as "an actors' opera"—intended, in other words, for actors who could sing rather than (as is usual) for singers who can't act.

We did this piece twice at Yale with a cast that included Alvin Epstein, Eugene Troobnick, George Gaynes, William Redfield, and Linda Lavin, all of them singing actors. To me, it was almost revolutionary in the way it broke down those stubborn walls traditionally erected between theatre and opera. I began to imagine some of the lighter Mozart operas—particularly *The Marriage of Figaro* and *Così Fan Tutte*, the musical comedies of their day—performed in a manner that would allow actors to bring their deeper character resources to lyric dramas that, in performance, are often musically exquisite but theatrically dead. Opera buffs, of course, will never be satisfied with anything less than the best-trained sopranos, coloraturas, tenors, baritones, and bassos. But it was my hope that we could compensate for deficiencies in musical artistry by helping to realize the deeper theatrical intentions of the work.

I have wandered a bit from my discussion of coaches and how they can help you become a better actor. But I am actually back to the same point I made earlier in my letter to you: Learn as much about your field as possible. The more skills you acquire, the more universal your talents will be and, in turn, the longer your life as an actor.

24

Actors and Critics

One day, some years ago, the great actress Colleen Dewhurst came to visit my Repertory Ideal class at the ART. The students asked her what she considered the most difficult thing about being an actor. She replied, "Vulnerability," and went on to explain that an actor is required to have a very thin skin if she is to enter the lives of characters other than her own, but the very quality that makes an actor sensitive to experience also makes her excessively vulnerable to insult and rejection.

I have never forgotten that remark. It is the actor's paradox and the artist's burden. If your skin is too porous, you will not survive very well in a world that does not care a fig about your feelings. If you develop too thick a protective crust, you will never be an artist.

This brings us to the weird symbiotic relationship that exists between the actor and the critic, two species with as much natural affinity as the mongoose and the snake (and there is no doubt about which one has the biggest lump in its throat). No one can protect you from the critic's barbs. In the course of your theatrical life, you will suffer wounds and lacerations, just like everyone else in the public eye. Because my position on both sides of the footlights has caused me to give as well as take lumps, I hope I can provide some guidance for you through this thorny thicket, or at least assure you that you are not alone.

The first drama critic, Aristotle, writing *The Poetics* in the fourth century B.C., did not have a lot to say about acting. His main concern was to create a definition of tragedy, with an emphasis on play construction, so that he could explain its powerful effect (known as catharsis) on the average spectator. It is true that he defined tragedy as "an imitation of an action," and imitation (or *mimesis*) is essentially the actor's function. But of the six elements of tragedy he names in descending order of importance, the first three are exclusively the playwright's business: plot (or *mythos*), character (or *ethos*), and theme (or *dianoia*). After this, in lowly fourth place, comes the actor's contribution—semantics, or diction—which probably means the kind of delivery taught in acting schools: rhetoric, intonation, syntax, and the like. Aristotle quickly passes over this as irrelevant to the playwright's art. (It might be of some consolation to know that Aristotle considered direction and scene design of even less importance.)

Aristotle is the first of many critics who, being writers themselves, have been largely concerned with the literary or written side of the theatre and less concerned with its histrionic aspect. And that may be another reason why he regards plot as more significant than character. How the actor interprets his or her role is of secondary importance to how the action of the play proceeds. (His minimizing of character may also have been his way of replying to Plato's belief that the major, perhaps the only, concern of art was to hold up ethical ideals of conduct, otherwise known as "good character.")

Aristotle thus started a tradition of criticism that, leaning heavily on theory, generally ignored the art of acting. If we except Gotthold Lessing, the first great drama critic, who covered German theatre in the eighteenth century, the profession of theatre reviewing did not really begin until the nineteenth century. The few accounts we have of performance before then generally come from audience members, one being Samuel Pepys's seventeenth-century account of playgoing in his celebrated *Diary*. Pepys totally missed the boat on *A Midsummer Night's Dream*, which he called "the most insipid ridiculous play" he had ever seen (though he admired the dancing and "the handsome women"). And although his *Poetics* suggests that Aristotle fully enjoyed watching the plays of Sophocles and Euripides on the stage, the theorists who followed him generally preferred the theatre in their heads.

I am suggesting that the anti-theatrical prejudice I described in an earlier letter has occasionally infected commentary on the theatre as well. Regarding the playwright as either the supreme artist or the chief miscreant of the theatrical event, it has led to a tradition that implicitly considers subsidiary figures, including actors and directors, as something of an obstacle to the direct experience of a play.

This attitude has colored a lot of scholarship, but it has also leeched out a little into the world of theatre reviewing. Eric Bentley, one of the finest critics of the twentieth century, was essentially a partisan of playwrights (notably George Bernard Shaw and Bertolt

Brecht) as you might guess from the title of his indispensable book, *The Playwright as Thinker.* And although he also has been interested in performance, which he chronicled in *In Search of Theatre*, and perhaps because he adapts and writes plays himself, he seems to have lost interest in experimental theatre, and has expressed particular dislike for conceptual directors (so, by the way, does my former student Michael Feingold of *The Village Voice*).

On the other hand, another breed of brilliant drama critics—George Bernard Shaw, Harold Clurman, Kenneth Tynan, for example—all had a passionate love of the theatre, and for actors in particular (for Shaw, this passion extended into a relationship with Mrs. Patrick Campbell). The best theatre critics, in fact, have usually been theatre people themselves—Shaw as a playwright, Clurman as a director, and Tynan as a compound of actor, scenario writer, literary director, and producer (he initiated the erotic revue *Oh! Calcutta*).

Of the three, Tynan was the least artistically gifted and he knew it. He once famously defined the critic as a man "who knows the way but can't drive the car." But when it came to acting, few knew the way better. His greatest gift as a critic, in fact, was not so much his taste in plays—indeed, he preferred John Osborne to Samuel Beckett, for example, and liked Brecht for all the wrong reasons—but his capacity to evoke, through a prose of extraordinary suppleness, the immediate act of performance. To read a Tynan review was almost to be present at the theatre event, as this sample of his notice of Olivier's *Titus Andronicus* attests:

> *This is a performance which ushers us into the presence of one who is, pound for pound, the greatest*

> *actor alive. As usual he raises one's hair with the risks he takes. Titus enters not as a beaming hero but as a battered veteran, stubborn and shambling, long past caring about people's cheers. A hundred campaigns have tanned his heart to leather, and from the creaking of that heart there issues a terrible music, not untinged by madness.*

Tynan's description tells us not only how Olivier's Titus looked and spoke, but about the underground movements of his heart. He wrote the kind of review that actually preserves the "illusion of the first time."

The same was true of his great predecessor, George Bernard Shaw. It was not his capacity to discover playwriting talent that made him an immortal critic. To be sure, he was a fervent champion of Ibsen and did much to bring his plays to England. But after Ibsen, his favorite playwright was the "unforgettable" (now forgotten) Henri Brieux, and Shaw's was the only wrongheaded notice of Oscar Wilde's masterpiece *The Importance of Being Earnest.* Shaw's strength was his moral and social passion, and his total dedication to the best theatrical art. His essay on the comparative merits of Sarah Bernhardt and Eleanora Duse when both were playing *Camille* (he preferred Duse's merging of herself with the character to Bernhardt's external display of personal "charm") is still a *locus classicus* of acting criticism. And he was the most versatile of observers. To go from music critic to theatre critic to playwright for Shaw was a smooth journey with no sudden stops or jerks along the way.

As for Clurman, this man was a performance in himself. It was not simply the way he dressed to go to the theatre—slouch hat, draped overcoat, and cane, and usually with an actress on his arm. It was the way he enthused about the stage. Clurman was not overwhelmed by "highbrow" works of art; he was attracted to "music, lights, scenery, beautiful girls," as he used to shout when lecturing theatre students, exhorting and gesticulating with such an excess of passion that one feared for his health. As a critic, Clurman knew actors from close up—by directing them, and by being married to them. His first wife was Stella Adler. And although the tempestuous relationship between these two large temperaments eventually ended in divorce, neither underestimated what each had taught the other.

I have singled out these three critics because, in a sense, they are so singular. The common run of "typewriters," as Clurman sometimes called his fellow scriveners on the aisle, have been much less understanding of the actor's craft, and less sympathetic to the actor's goals. There are two primary explanations for this, apart from a simple lack of sensibility—lack of time and lack of space. The large majority of the critical fraternity writes for newspapers and television. Print reviewers are required to pound out their curt notices in just a few hours, and television commentators are limited to sound bites of less than a minute, perhaps extended by a brief thirty-second scene from the production.

Under such circumstances, it is no wonder that the typical drama review, in daily newspapers and on network television, is largely an expression of opinion. The expansive descriptive writing of Shaw and Clurman and Tynan was written for weeklies—the *Saturday Review*, the *Nation*, the *Observer*, and the *New Yorker*—which allowed them more time for reflection, research, and composition, and a lot more words with which to exercise their prose style. But these critics were writing for theatre enthusiasts, even (they secretly hoped) for posterity. Reviewers write for the average consumer and for the box office over which they exercise an unprecedented influence. In most American cities, one newspaper can determine whether a production lives or dies. In what other art form do critics have such power?

Undoubtedly under pressure from editors, the daily critic is required to deliver a snap judgment that precludes any true confrontation with a play or a production, much less a considered evaluation of the acting, largely for the purpose of guiding tourists towards the latest hit and away from the latest flop.

This kind of writing I have elsewhere called "Himalaya Criticism," after a remark by Danny Kaye who, when asked how he liked the Himalayas, replied, "Loved him. Hated her." Thumbs up, thumbs down. You can imagine what it is like, if you have not yet had the experience, to prepare a part for weeks, rehearse it for months, and then have your performance summed up in one day, provided you're noticed at all, with a brief judgmental phrase—"X was stunning in the part of Clarence," "Y sailed down the Nile and sank," or "Z runs the gamut of emotions from A to B" (all from actual reviews). That splendid, highly intelligent British actor, Diana Rigg, has edited a collection of this type of notice in her book, *No Turn Unstoned.* It is proof that theatre writers over the ages have been much more infatuated with their own opinions than with the object under review.

Not all reviewers are always so abrupt or dismissive. In my own city of Boston, for example, Elliot Norton of the *Boston Herald* was deeply respected because, without ever lowering his standards, his reviews were so obviously designed to help improve a production rather than destroy it. The other major local reviewer, Kevin ("Killer") Kelly of the *Boston Globe*, on the other hand, wrote notices that were typically so vituperative that many Broadway producers stopped bringing their shows to Boston, and the city lost its position as a tryout center for New York. Unfortunately, it was the Himalaya criticism of Kelly, not the process-sensitive approach of Norton, that became the model for local theatre reviewing.

Such criticism has its admirers, but it can spread havoc through a theatre community. My late first wife was an actress, and I know from personal experience that a bad notice can sometimes be fatal. On countless occasions, after someone in my company has been hammered by an unfair and thoughtless review, I have felt obliged to call the actor and find some way to ease the pain.

Some time ago, when the two-time Academy Award winner Luise Rainer performed a one-woman show *(Enoch Arden)* at the ART, Kevin Kelly took the occasion to review not her acting so much as the way she had aged (he was particularly graphic about wrinkles, wattles, and blemishes). Luise had one more performance to give, and I feared that if she read that notice she would not be able to go on stage. At a reception preceding that final show, some thoughtless soul handed her a copy of the review, which Luise kept in her hand unread while talking with some admirers. I told her manager to get the wretched thing away from her or there would be no show, and he deftly removed it from her grasp while whispering some instructions in her ear. The final show went on. I still do not know whether she ever read the review.

Some actors claim that they never read reviews ("So have I heard and do in part believe," says Shakespeare's skeptic Horatio). If this is true, it is because reviews can be so shocking to the system, so wounding to the ego. Why should actors be more sensitive to criticism than other mortals? Because, as I have already suggested, they are the only artists who function as their own instruments. The writer has his book, the painter her canvas, the composer his concerto, the musician her violin or piano, the singer his voice, the dancer her feet—all the actor has is himself or herself. Reject that and you create a condition of vulnerability that is similar to ripping the clothes off one's soul.

But what about the actor's roles, you will ask, the parts he plays, the lines she speaks. Aren't those a buffer between the critique and the self? Yes, to some extent they are. And it is also true that nontheatrical artists can be as sensitive to criticism as actors. Writers, for example, have been known to commit assault and battery on hostile critics, sometimes with intent to maim or kill. But there is no question that the actor identifies with his or her role much more intensely than, say, the singer or the dancer. That is why "personalization" is the very essence of the major acting systems. Love me, love my role.

Perhaps this explains why most people, including reviewers, display such passionate feelings towards actors. Critics like to admit they are as "stage-struck" as any other theatergoer. They have often been known to "lose their hearts," to "fall head over heels," "to be madly infatuated," to quote some of the hyperbole used in their reviews. Harold Clurman was not the only critic to be seen at openings with a beautiful actress on his arm, or to be married to one. So was George Jean Nathan. Such is the image of the critic in the popular imagination. Think of the way Addison deWitt (George Sanders) squired and mentored the ambitious Eve Harrington (Anne Baxter) in *All About Eve.*

Yet, paradoxically, it remains an unwritten law among aisle-sitters that reviewers should not fraternize with theatre people, and especially with actors. They fear that the qualities they value most—detachment, impersonality, impartiality—will somehow be affected by getting to know someone they might later review, either at a dinner or a cocktail party. This is a pity for several reasons. Chief among them is that more familiarity with knowledgeable theatre artists would make reviewers better informed about their field. As Olivier once suggested: "Critics should be encouraged to sit in on rehearsals so that they could see the amount of work, concentration, belief and love that goes into the construction of a piece, before they take their inky swords to it." It might also make them less likely to yield to the greatest temptation and besetting sin of critics, namely, to be witty at somebody else's expense, to use their literary skills to ridicule those who work on stage.

Savage criticism has always been a scourge of the profession, and all of us have been guilty of using it on occasion. But there is no question that it reached its apogee in recent times with John Simon, who writes for *New York* magazine. Now I have known Simon for many years. Indeed, I helped get him his earliest jobs as a reviewer. He is a brilliant scholar and a lively writer. But once having caught the attention of the public with his more brutal reviews, he seemed to recognize that it was bull-goring, bear-baiting, and pig-sticking, rather than reflective thinking, that made a drama critic popular these days.

Simon's evolution into the Transylvanian vampire of *New York* Magazine made him famous for a while.

Readers enjoyed watching him take pot shots at any moving object, actors being the most conspicuous and targetable. He was not above expressing his disgust at the "flipper-like limbs" or "uberous left breast" of some helpless actress whose personal appearance, regardless of her acting ability, somehow violated his aesthetic sensibilities. American theatre, for Simon at his worst, seemed to be a montage of glazed eyes, bulging warts, bad skin, wrinkled necks, and rotten teeth.

There is no adequate defense against this kind of criticism. One of Simon's victims, Sylvia Miles, once poured a plate of spaghetti over his head at a restaurant, which is, I suppose, a kind of defense. But the only way to deal with hurtful reviews is to remember that today's newspaper is tomorrow's refuse. The best response to intemperate criticism I know was made by a nineteenth-century German composer in reply to a music critic who had panned his latest symphony. He wrote: "Sir! I am sitting in the smallest room in my house. I have your review before me. Soon it will be behind me." Another equally appropriate (if equally crude) response can be found in a cartoon I sometimes use on my notepad. Captioned "The Critic," it shows a tiny little man standing behind a very substantial, voluptuous, and naked woman on all fours, the word "ART" written on her ample buttocks. He is in the act of unbuttoning his fly.

Simon, for all his fulminating, has never had much impact on the American theatre one way or another. But he helped create a legacy (inherited by Dale Peck in literary criticism and by Bill O'Reilly and Sean Hannity in television commentary) in which insult, abuse, and humiliation became the hallmarks of style. Inevitably, Simon's influence has been felt on other theatre reviewers, even those in the *New York Times*. Compare the dignified gravitas of Brooks Atkinson with the occasionally dismissive style of his successor, Frank Rich, and you may detect the shadow of John Simon in Times Square. In his poem on the death of W. B. Yeats, W. H. Auden pleads with the dead poet to "teach the free man how to praise." It is a lesson all critics must learn again and again, myself included.

Yet, if criticism can be too harsh, it can also be too charitable. The flip side of excessive censure is excessive flattery. Since one of the obligations of Himalaya criticism is to create hits and invent stars, this results in a species of puffing that can undermine a reviewer's credibility. Pick up a newspaper on any day of the week and look at the theatre ads. The critical quotes read like advertising copy. Indeed, many of them are written to serve as advertising copy. This is partly the result of vanity (the reviewer's ambition to be quoted in the ads), partly the result of necessity (the reviewer's understanding that productions will not survive without exaggerated praise). Of course, no theatre producer is going to object to such hyperbole as "Best damn play I ever saw" or "The funniest play on Broadway" or "The most powerful show of the season," or to any of the other superlatives that stud the theatre marquees. And no Broadway stars will be offended by the kind of starry-eyed adjectives that are showered on their performances. But in some ways this sort of thing can be just as damaging to an artist as a savage notice.

I have mentioned those two major sources of critical shortcomings, space and time. For many years, morning newspaper reviewers had to start their notices right after the curtain came down and complete them in time for the morning edition. That kind of operation took a special kind of talent, one that few people possess. I certainly do not have it, so when the *Times* asked me to be their drama reviewer in 1966, I had no alternative but to decline (I also did not want to be responsible for the potential unemployment of so many hardworking theatre people). I recommended my colleague on the *New Republic*, the film critic Stanley Kauffmann, for the job. He lasted one season. But Kauffmann accomplished one important thing during his brief tenure at the *Times*, and this despite the initial howls of Broadway producers: He managed to gain permission for reviewers to see shows during previews, rather than on opening nights, to allow more time for writing.

This development had some effect on the quality of critical prose. It had no effect on the quality of critical judgment. Regardless of the longer time available for reflection and writing, reviewers were still rating the Himalayas rather than trying to describe them or climb them, still providing consumer reports for the audience rather than useful information for the theatre person. This was true of even the best writers for the *Times* after Kauffmann left—notably Walter Kerr and Frank Rich.

Kerr was a man of the theatre and a highly admired stylist. Before he joined the *Herald-Tribune* and later the *Times*, first as daily reviewer, then as Sunday reviewer, he had taught drama at Catholic University, had written criticism for *Commonweal*, and had even composed the book for a Broadway musical. Broadway producers found him to be the most sympathetic and most theatre savvy of all the daily reviewers. Indeed, my friend and former student Rocco Landesman, president of Jujamcyn, even renamed one of his theatres after him.

Like the majority of reviewers, however, Kerr was more interested in playwriting than in performance, though he wrote a fine book on silent film acting called *The Silent Clowns.* Partly because of his own aesthetic, partly because of his strict Catholic upbringing, he disliked most of the great playwrights of the modern period, including Ibsen, Strindberg, Chekhov, and Brecht. And he famously called Beckett's *Waiting for Godot* "out of touch with the hearts and minds of the folks out front." But his analysis of plays was never less than intelligent, and his prose was always supple.

Nourished as he was on commercial Broadway fare, however, he totally failed to understand the process of performance in the not-for-profit theatre. It was for that reason that we tried, in the early years of the Yale Repertory Theatre, to protect our actors from his premature judgments. I have already mentioned how hard it was to evolve a permanent acting company under the harsh and judgmental glare of New York criticism. I feared the same kind of premature judgment could kill a company in nearby New Haven.

That is precisely why Tyrone Guthrie elected to form the Minnesota Theatre Company (later known as the Guthrie Theatre) in Minneapolis. If he could not keep the New York critics away entirely, at least he could keep them at a distance and thus mitigate the harm they might do to his fledgling company. After Walter Kerr came up to New Haven to review our production of *Prometheus Bound*—quite favorably, I might add—I wrote a letter to the *Times:* "We're grateful for the review. We hope he never comes again. Whether he liked it or not, I felt it was a mistake for him to cover the play, thereby imposing upon us the hit-or-miss pressure of Broadway."

Kerr tolerated my early appeals not to review our work at Yale, though he correctly criticized my brash tone ("I will respect your wishes," he wrote, "I wish I could respect your manners"). But we came from opposite sides of the aesthetic spectrum, so he and I had not been exactly friendly colleagues during the pre-Yale years when I was reviewing for *The New Republic.* In fact, I had once half-seriously proposed to stop covering Broadway if he would give up reviewing off-Broadway and what I took to be his insensitive treatment of the not-for-profit theatre (more bad manners!).

My guilty secret is that I have a history of quarrelling with the majority critics, particularly on the *Times*, first when I was a critic myself and later when I became an artistic director. The Yale actors were not happy about my position, for understandable reasons. Most of them wanted their work covered in the national press. You need the quotes for your resume, especially if you are planning to leave the relatively cloistered confines of a resident company and you don't want to alienate people you might need in future. Because our first Yale company included some very well-known actors—among them Stacey Keach, Harris Yulin, Kenneth Haigh, Ron Leibman, Estelle Parsons, Kathleen Widdoes, and Richard Jordan—I seemed to be dooming them to temporary obscurity during their time in New Haven.

You might well ask why I, a critic myself, and not always a very gentle one, should, as an artistic director, have been so hostile to criticism during my company's formative years. Well, the easy answer is that, critics being as sensitive to criticism as artists are, sometimes even more, I was partly trying to protect myself. But another truth is that immersing oneself in company work makes you much more sensitive to the delicate process of how works of art evolve, and much more conscious of how a hasty judgment can damage and even kill the creative mechanism. Along with Olivier, I recommend some time with a company in one capacity or other for every drama reviewer.

Despite our increasing foundation support, my own principles about the New York press were soon to be tested by our growing dependence on the box office. And the box office, alas, was highly sensitive to reviews, especially those in the *New York Times.* After about ten years, I would be begging Walter Kerr to visit our productions, which he treated with the same quizzical, slightly patronizing tone he applied to any work that ventured beyond the familiar and the accepted.

His review of our *Midsummer Night's Dream*, for example, though he called the production "among the most beautiful I have ever seen on any stage," didn't even mention its primary artist, Alvin Epstein. Further, it did not recognize this production as the work of an ongoing resident theatre. I asked our dramaturg, Michael Feingold, later the principal critic for the *Village Voice*, to respond to Kerr this time. In his letter to the *Times*, he wrote:

> *To attend a permanent theatre institution and single out "elements" of production is as useless as isolating the production itself without reference to the other works in the repertory; it is to ignore the fact that each person's work, and each production, has value only in the service of a larger idea than itself, that it is merely a step in a company's life, another muscle tensed for an even greater leap in future.*

Neither cheeky letters like this one nor my own cantankerous correspondence were designed to endear us to the reviewers, and it could be argued that our company actors suffered from such behavior. On the other hand, there was no reason why people in the theatre had to suffer the slings and arrows of outrageous critics without at least making themselves heard.

For a while, the *Times* had a section called "Backtalk," a forum through which theatre people could respond to what they considered unfair criticism. But that idea, like the notion of employing a daily and a Sunday critic on the same paper who might even disagree with each other, was soon to be discarded. Whenever I got the opportunity, I would suggest to newspaper editors, particularly on the *Times*, that they hire two daily critics and run their reviews side by side as a reminder to readers that a production could inspire different opinions, including their own. But the *Times* was never willing to demythologize its drama critic, nor to loosen its stranglehold on the New York theatre. In the past, Broadway was ruled by seven newspaper critics. Now its fate was entirely in the hands of one, just as one newspaper ruled the theatre in virtually every other major city in the land. This kind of empowerment was not only deleterious to the theatre, it was destructive to the reviewer, for if power corrupts, as Lord Acton correctly observed, absolute power corrupts absolutely.

Kerr was succeeded on the *Times* by Clive Barnes, Richard Eder, and Frank Rich. They all, perhaps Rich more than the others, exemplified Acton's axiom, and I let them all know it. Indeed, Frank Rich became perhaps the most powerful drama critic in *Times* history, occupying that role from 1980 until 1993. Eventually, he moved to the editorial page in his new role as op-ed columnist, and thence to the "Arts and Leisure" section with a culturally oriented political column. But he still retains some influence over the paper's theatre policies, including, it is said, the choice of his successor.

Rich is an excellent writer with a lively and urbane mind, driven by a powerful political passion. The problem is not with his liberal politics, with which I am often in agreement, nor is it with his graceful style, which I admire. Rather, it is that the humane attitudes he now expresses towards the victims of political oppression never seemed to extend towards the victims of his reviews. Like his critical mentor, John Simon, he made the wounding of defenseless theatre people a source of gladiatorial entertainment. As a result, a whole species of experimental theatre, and a host of fine stage artists—among them the playwrights Christopher Durang and Arthur Kopit, the directors Andrei Serban and JoAnne Akalaitis, and countless actors—were for a while in virtual exile from the New York stage.

We tried various ways of confronting the issue of theatre criticism over the years. One solution at Yale was to initiate a critic's program leading to a doctor of fine arts degree for the sake of improving the quality and kind of contemporary drama criticism. The DFA students were encouraged to see as many productions as possible, and even to start reviewing the ones we presented at Yale. We believed that if critics were better informed about the process of performance, they would be better prepared for the profession of making judgments.

The new species we were trying to create I called (in an essay of the same name) "The Repertory Critic." With the development of so many resident companies throughout the country, the theatre had changed. Shouldn't criticism change as well? The commercial theatre believed that the function of criticism was to provide space in the print and broadcast media for selling their shows. The resident theatres, though also eager for positive reviews and frequent features, were equally interested in the reflective aspect of the critical process in helping to improve its work. Could criticism be a medium of thought as well as of entertainment, a form of analysis as well as of publicity and advertising?

For actors, this would mean an observer out front capable of observing performance not as an isolated event in an isolated show but rather as a continuum, a progress of theatre artists from production to production under the auspices of company work. Such a critic would share the audience's capacity to appreciate how an actor transformed from role to role, from play to play, and how that actor developed and grew from year to year. In short, the repertory critic would not be adjudicating hits and flops so much as judging the design and purpose of the whole. This type of critic could also be the conscience of an institution, noting when it fell short of its declared ideals, when it compromised its identity and for what reasons.

A few such critics were already around—notably Jack Kroll of *Newsweek*, William Henry III of *Time*, Don Shewey of the *Village Voice*, and, Mel Gussow of the *New York Times*. But because most of the more intelligent writers lacked either the carfare or the ambition to venture very far outside of New York, my call for repertory critics largely went unheeded. Even our effort to create a few at Yale was unsuccessful. It was daunting how quickly the students in criticism fell into established patterns of conduct. The postproduction critique was sometimes so immoderate that it became known as the "blood bath," our actors protesting that they were being exposed to attacks from within their own precincts. It was not the last time I was to hear these complaints.

We discontinued the program after a few years, partly because the criticism students were being demonized, and even ostracized, as internal enemies, and partly because they were not very successful in obtaining employment after graduation. Michael Feingold was an exception, and there were others as well, usually working for the alternative press. But for the most part, it became clear that the major newspapers did not want a well-prepared reviewer writing for educated theatergoers and intelligent professionals. They preferred someone who could guide the taste of the lowest common denominator of their readership. Consumer criticism was to remain well-entrenched within the borders of the third estate.

Another effort to influence the nature of drama criticism took place in the summer of 1992 at Harvard, in collaboration with the Nieman Foundation in Journalism. I had always been opposed to including quotes from critics in our ads, partly out of the belief that if you validated their praise, you were also obliged to endorse their dispraise. The ART management was convinced that quotes were the quickest way to sell a show. I believed a nonprofit institution was required to explore avenues different from those of the commercial theatre, even in its publicity and advertising. If, as on Broadway, our survival was going to be determined by critical reviews, then we were back in the brothel. I persuaded the Mellon Foundation to help me test my theories by providing a grant that would (1) insure us against loss if we dropped all critical quotes from our ads; (2) underwrite a conference on criticism to explore alternative possibilities; and (3) provide remuneration for scholars and intellectuals (none of them professional theatre critics) to review our plays in the pages of our own newsletter. All these proposals created fireworks.

The commissioning of nonprofessional commentators was another of my efforts to raise the intelligence quotient of drama criticism. I thought that if we could attract informed scholars such as Christopher Ricks or Stephen Greenblatt or Harold Bloom to write reviews or serve on panels, we could not only benefit from their literary knowledge but also provide them with the opportunity to think about the production process. Howls of pain from our actors and directors. It was bad enough, they argued, to be forced to endure the lash of outside critics. But to invite them inside as well, as moles in our own newsletter, was an act of masochism. The few reviews we published, even when negative, were among the best informed we ever received. And I still think the idea a good one. But out of respect for members of the company, I gave it up after publishing a few articles.

If the guest reviewing raised internal protest, the weekend conference raised protest from without, particularly from those critics who had not been invited. Still, it served its major function, which was to provide the occasion for the lion to lie down with the lamb. The conference was an opportunity for critics to meet theatre people, including some of the actors, directors, and playwrights they had criticized, and for theatre people to air their disagreements with critics in a relatively congenial atmosphere.

The meeting was doomed to turn confrontational. Following an amiable keynote address by Benedict

Nightingale, former Sunday critic for the *New York Times*, the blood began to flow. Frank Rich had been invited but declined—no doubt wisely, because he was destined to be one of the major targets. There was, for example, a backstage feud going on between him and Jack Kroll of *Newsweek* (whom Rich had anointed with the title "Jack-the-Hype"), which Kroll took the opportunity to air in public. Jules Feiffer took bitter exception to John Simon's exceptional bitterness, and both engaged in an exchange of insults rarely seen outside of *Hardball* and *The O'Reilly Factor.* Kevin Kelly of the *Boston Globe*, perhaps because he hadn't been invited, would reserve his own nasty comments for future reviews of our work.

A lot of my attempt to change the nature of criticism, was, I admit, quixotic, if not counterproductive. We really had no hope of reforming a system that had been entrenched for years, largely for economic reasons, and you can't argue with the profit motive. On the other hand, I was upset by how helpless theatre people were in the face of sometimes gratuitous insult, and by the way this helplessness sometimes exacerbated the reviewer's spleen. Rather than watch someone suffer with his leg in a trap, I thought even a small expression of protest was preferable to silence, and it made some of us feel a little better for a while. When the Mellon grant ran out, I was reluctantly persuaded by management that the absence of quotes in our ads was seriously affecting sales, and feeling a little like General Lee surrendering at Appomattox, I agreed to revert to the old ways. But I never regretted the attempt, and I do not think we suffered much in the long run.

Was there any benefit to be had from my incorrigible baiting of reviewers? Was I doing our company more harm than good? There is no question that I was in a no-win situation, that the critics held all the trumps, and that perfectly innocent people were probably suffering for my indulgences. So, by the way, was I. I was not surprised when the former editor of the *Times*'s Arts and Leisure section, an old friend of mine, revealed that, although I had been a frequent contributor to the paper, it was blackballing me as a writer, and ignoring the YRT as a theatre. Later, after I had complained about the arts criticism of the *Boston Globe* in an article called "As the Globe Turns," it was obvious that Kevin Kelly's reviews of the ART were also becoming seriously skewed.

With the changing of the editorial guard both at the *Times* and the *Globe*, these restraints were eventually lifted and peace returned to our company. And although I was never entirely happy with the way our actors were written about, at least the sources of acrimony had been removed. I guess the moral of this letter—one I have never learned myself—is that, as far as the critics are concerned, you must shut up and take your lumps. Or as Olivier advised us in his book on acting: "Do not despair when the hand of criticism plunges into your body and claws at your soul; you must endure it, accept it, and smile."

25

Ephemeris, Ephemeris

I believe the reason theatre people respond so strongly to theatre criticism is that it represents one of the few extant records of performance. This means that your entire professional existence may be validated not by your work, which disappears, but by people's opinions about it. For let it be said at once, the most painful thing about an actor's life is its impermanence. Playwrights have their printed or typed texts. Composers have their scores and CDs. Designers have their models and sketches, their photos of sets and costumes. What the actor has, once the performance is over, is memories and air. Having been an actor for a short time himself, Kenneth Tynan realized how unfair it was "that an art so potent should also be so transient." That is one of the reasons he accepted the challenge to perpetuate it in print.

In David Mamet's play, *A Life in the Theatre*, two actors, one young, the other old, share a dressing room. The younger man, John, looks forward to new achievements; the elder, Robert, looks back on what he has already accomplished. And when Robert stands on stage and turns his eyes on the empty house, the only words he can murmur are "Ephemeris, ephemeris." All the roles he has played—ephemeral. The relationships he may have established with the audience—ephemeral. The relationship the two actors have established with each other—ephemeral. All that is left of a "life in the theatre" are "the bars, the houses, the drafty halls. The pencilled scripts. . . . It all goes so fast. It all goes so quickly."

Nothing mirrors the fleeting, fugitive nature of life more vividly than its representation upon the stage. How can we hold on to those precious moments as long as possible before they fade away?

Of course, there are photographs, and almost every actor keeps a photograph album. If these are candid shots, they may have a touch of spontaneity. If posed and frozen, they are just another form of artificiality. Still, photographs are better than nothing. The moment-to-moment energy of performance may be lost, but at least a moment has been preserved. Photos can sometimes substitute for the oil portraits of yesteryear (several of which still hang in New York's Player's Club) when painters tried to capture a great actor on the cusp of a great performance.

And then there is videotape. Two problems arise with this kind of record, however. The first is that Actors Equity has imposed severe restrictions on the way video cameras can be used in the theatre. It is understandable why the actors union should want to protect its membership from unpaid presentations of their work. But for years, it refused management permission to record anything more than a few minutes of a show for publicity purposes. Some years ago, Equity relented and agreed to let a theatre videotape an entire show, but only for the use of the stage managers. The purpose was to preserve the blocking for understudies and replacements. The guidelines were strict. Only one camera could be in place, in a fixed position (though zooming was permitted). And there could be no public presentation of the tape, not even for educational use, on pain of severe penalties from the union.

As a result, hundreds of thousands of marvelous performances have been lost, or preserved in a form that destroys the original magic. On the other hand, there is one important compensation for such a loss, namely, that the performance continues to live in the memory banks of the audience for whom it was originally created rather than in a medium for which it was never intended. It can be painful to see on tape a show one loved on stage, the dimly perceived actors reduced to distant images on a flat screen. That was why I was so excited when WGBH decided to record our production of *A Midsummer Night's Dream* for national television. At last, we would have a chance to preserve a work of ours in its entirety and in its original form.

The entire show was televised on the stage of the Wilbur Theatre in Boston under the auspices of an excellent television director, Richard Heller. This was a theatrical event being performed before a live audience, and no effort was made to hide that. Recorded on two separate performances, the camera captured the audience's reactions, both visually and aurally, panning over their heads for close-ups of the actors with no attempt to hide their sweat and their greasepaint. Some network executives complained that the event was not true television, that the production should have been transferred to a studio. But for me, this was one of the few times in history that one medium deferred to the strengths of another and did not try to compete with it.

Another of our successes, Serban's version of Molière's *Sganarelle*, actually was adapted for television by England's Channel 4 on the stage of the Duke of York Theatre in London. It used a studio set, it cut the play, and it was, to my mind, an embarrassment. All the magic of the event had evaporated, turned into mere sleight of hand. The performances had lost the vital energy that can only be stimulated by a live audience. To this day, I cannot watch that show on video. I want to remember it as an authentic stage performance, not as a canned reproduction.

But perhaps the best way to preserve performance in the theatre is through repertory. Just as opera and dance companies store the costumes, sets, and prompt books of former productions in warehouses for later presentation, so the American theatre has once again begun to realize that it can keep past shows alive, in the same way, for future audiences. A successful production from one season can always be remounted during the next. Indeed, you can even re-stage a popular show as much as ten or twenty years later. My production of *Six Characters in Search of an Author* actually became a signature of the ART, played in repertory first 1984, and fourteen years later in repertory with Gozzi's *The King Stag*. True, the actors would change from time to time as the years went on. For example, the six-year-old who played the Little Girl in the original production, Nicole Shalhoub, is now twenty-five and has just graduated from the acting program of the ART Institute. But the spirit of the production still lives, and this is one of the best things I can say about repertory theatre.

True, this method preserves the show rather than the individual performance, so one can understand, therefore, why even the most dedicated stage actor would want to make movies. Regardless of how little you may control the final product, at least some aspect of your performance is perpetuated on celluloid. The trouble is that you may not want it perpetuated there.

I know many film actors who cannot bear to look at their old movies, and I think I understand why. Something of you is fading in those performances that cannot be recaptured or held. Imagine what it would be like if, say, Paul Muni or Sylvia Sidney, typical of the fine old actors of the 1930s who left the stage for Hollywood, were to return from the dead and find the only record of their work in such films as *Scarface* and *Dead End.* Imagine how they would wince at the crackling sound track, the breaks in the celluloid, and, particularly, their own high-pitched voices and overemotional acting. How much better to preserve the memory of their achievements in the minds of their admirers.

Another disadvantage of preserving performance on film has to do with the passage of time. The invention of celluloid has given recent generations the dubious advantage of watching their acting heroes deteriorate before their very eyes. Movies have the unusual capacity to freeze an animated moment in time; they also have the unpleasant capacity, when seen sequentially, to capture the ravages of time. This was not true of James Mason, for example, who seemed to be a young man until the day he died, or of Cary Grant, who showed no significant sign of aging over the years except for his snowy hair. But the passage of time, and his own physical disorders, turned my idol Olivier into a human being entirely different from the one he was during his days as a swarthy brooding leading man in *Wuthering Heights* as compared with the one he became in his later days as a decrepit Jewish refugee in *The Boys from Brazil* or as an aging Nazi dentist in *Marathon Man.* Those changes are much more difficult to detect in the theatre.

So, dear Actor, in some strange way the ephemeral nature of the theatre is one of its greatest consolations. How many times people have said that their best memories of acting are of past moments on the stage: Olivier's piercing offstage shriek as Oedipus when he discovered that he was the culprit plaguing Thebes; Helene Weigel's "silent scream" in *Mother Courage* when she disguises her agony while her child is being executed; Laurette Taylor's desperate mincing as Amanda in Tennessee William's *The Glass Menagerie;* Alfred Lunt's uncontrollable vomiting in Peter Brooks's production of Friedrich Dürrenmatt's *The Visit*, upon realizing that he was about to be sacrificed to a community's greed; Madeleine Renaud's chirrupy optimism in Beckett's *Happy Days* as the earth rose farther and farther up her neck; Jason Robards's astonished desperation in *The Iceman Cometh* when he realized that exposing his friends' "pipe dreams" was not making them any happier; Jefferson Mays's impersonation of forty different on-stage characters in *I Am My Own Wife*, each with his or her own distinctive personalities.

Everyone has his own long list of great stage moments. These are the times when the theatre achieves its finest purpose as a vessel for carrying the terrors, hopes, delights, and aspirations we all share. These are the moments, dear Actor, that enhance the lives of the audiences, the moments that only you can bring to fulfillment. And these are the moments for which you initially chose the stage, the moments when our eyes remain steadfastly fixed on you.

26

Epilogue

I leave you with this, my dear young friend. I only hope you enjoy your life in the theatre as much as I have enjoyed mine. And I pray you never lose faith in the value of your calling. You have chosen to create when so many others are dedicated to destruction. With half the world devoted to death, you remain dedicated to life. The stories you enact on stage often involve some of the greatest fictional creations in literature written in the most incomparable language. They are myths of comedy and absurdity, heroism and crime, mayhem and terror. And people may well ask why, with so much terrorism in the world, anyone would want to see more terror on the stage. The answer is, of course, that the actor makes these terrifying stories transcendent, partly by making them comprehensible, partly by leavening the terror with pity. That is the reason audiences will continue to visit the theatre to see you, dear Actor, the living embodiment of their joys and fears.

Acknowledgments

The author wishes to thank Jan and Jeremy Geidt, and Rob Orchard, for their creative fact checking; Marilyn Plotkins for her exhaustive research; Megan Hustad for her editorial acumen; Jennifer Blakebrough-Raeburn for her sensitive copyediting; Daniel Brustein for his always loving encouragement; and Doreen Beinart for her loyalty, patience, and tolerance for a writer often cranky at his labors. Also thanks to the many actors who have taught me that the life of the theatre begins in the dressing room.

About the Author

Robert Brustein is a playwright, adaptor, director, actor, teacher, and critic. He is a Senior Research Fellow at Harvard University, the drama critic for the *New Republic*, and a former Dean of the Yale Drama School. Mr. Brustein was the founding director of the Yale Repertory Theatre and the American Repertory Theatre, and served for twenty-three years as Director of the Loeb Drama Center. He retired from the Artistic Directorship in 2002 and now serves as Founding Director and Creative Consultant for the American Repertory Theatre.

Robert Brustein is the author of thirteen books on theatre and society, including *Reimagining American Theatre*, *The Theatre of Revolt*, *Making Scenes* (a memoir of his Yale years), *Who Needs Theatre* (a collection of reviews and essays), *Dumbocracy in America*, and *Cultural Calisthenics*. His latest book, *The Siege of the Arts*, was released in 2001.

He has supervised more than two hundred productions, acting in eight and directing twelve, including his own adaptations of *The Father*, *Ghosts*, *The Changeling*, and the trilogy of Pirandello works: *Six Characters in*

Search of an Author, *Right You Are (If You Think You Are)*, and *Tonight We Improvise*. He is the author of *Nobody Dies on Friday*, and he adapted the musicals of *Shlemiel The First* and *Lysistrata*. His new play, *Spring Forward, Fall Back*, will be produced in New York in 2005.

Mr. Brustein has been elected to the American Academy of Arts and Letters and the American Academy of Arts and Sciences, and was recently inducted into the Theatre Hall of Fame. In 2002–2003, he was a Senior Fellow with the National Arts Journalism Program at Columbia University.

Index